There must be a shift in society's attitude

towards treating older people with dignity

and respect.

Sir Michael Parkinson, Dignity Ambassador

Royal College of Occupational Therapists

WITHDRAWN

UNEQUAL AGEING

The untold story of exclusion in old age

Edited by Paul Cann and Malcolm Dean

This edition published in Great Britain in 2009 by

The Policy Press
University of Bristol
Fourth Floor
Beacon House
Queen's Road
Bristol BS8 1QU
UK

Tel +44 (0)117 331 4054
Fax +44 (0)117 331 4093
e-mail tpp-info@bristol.ac.uk
www.policypress.co.uk

North American office:
The Policy Press
c/o International Specialized Books Services (ISBS)
920 NE 58th Avenue, Suite 300
Portland, OR 97213-3786, USA
Tel +1 503 287 3093
Fax +1 503 280 8832
e-mail info@isbs.com

British Library Cataloguing in Publication Data
A catalogue record for this book is available from the British Library.

Library of Congress Cataloging-in-Publication Data
A catalog record for this book has been requested.

ISBN 978 1 84742 411 2 paperback
ISBN 978 1 84742 412 9 hardcover

Cover design by The Policy Press
Front cover: image kindly supplied by Simon Wheatley/Magnum
Printed and bound in Great Britain by Hobbs the Printers, Southampton

Contents

List of tables and figures

Tables

Figures

Notes on contributors

Sue Adams is the Director of Care & Repair England, a national charity established in 1986 to improve the housing and living conditions of older people and people with disabilities. Sue is the independent co-chair of the government's advisory committee on housing and older people (Housing and Older People Development Group, or HOPDEV) and worked closely with Communities and Local Government on the housing strategy for an ageing society, *Lifetime homes, lifetime neighbourhoods*. She has served on a range of research and policy advisory groups, including the government's review of Disabled Facilities Grants and the Countryside Agency/Housing Corporation research into older people, housing and rural issues. She is the author and co-author of many publications and articles about older people and housing and is a fellow of the World Demographic Association.

Bryan Appleyard attended King's College, Cambridge, then worked at *The Times* as Financial News Editor and Deputy Arts Editor from 1976 to 1984. Since then he has been a freelance journalist, becoming Feature Writer of the Year three times and commended four times in the British Press Awards. He is currently a special feature writer, commentator, reviewer and columnist for *The Sunday Times*. His books include: *The culture club: Crisis in the arts*; *Richard Rogers: A biography*; *The pleasures of peace: Art and imagination in postwar Britain*; *Understanding the present: Science and the soul of modern man*; *Brave new worlds: Genetics and the human experience*; *Aliens: Why they are here* and *How to live forever or die trying: On the new immortality*. He has lectured, debated or taught at numerous universities, including Boston, St Andrews, Glasgow, Leeds, Cambridge, Oxford, Trinity College, Dublin, London, Liverpool John Moores, the Architectural Association, and the Glasgow School of Architecture, and has been a fellow of the World Economic Forum.

Paul Cann was Director of Policy, Research and International Development at Help the Aged from 2000 to 2009, with responsibility for research, policy and international strategy. He is now Chief Executive of Age Concern Oxfordshire. After reading English literature at King's College Cambridge, he taught for five years, then joined the Civil Service, where he held a range of postings at the Cabinet Office, including working as a Private Secretary to successive Cabinet ministers. A subsequent spell in the private sector included working for *The Independent* newspaper. He joined the charity world in 1992 as

Director of the British Dyslexia Association and subsequently of the National Autistic Society. He was a trustee of Contact a Family, a charity supporting carers and people with special needs or disabilities, and is now an Associate Fellow of the International Longevity Centre.

Anna Coote is Head of Social Policy at the New Economics Foundation (nef). A leading analyst, writer and advocate in the field of social policy, she has been Commissioner for Health with the UK Sustainable Development Commission since 2000. She was Director of Health Policy at The King's Fund from 1998 to 2004 before joining the Healthcare Commission to lead their work on engaging patients and the public (2005–08). Earlier posts include Senior Research Fellow and Deputy Director of the Institute for Public Policy Research (ippr) from 1989 to 1998, editor and producer of current affairs television for Diverse Productions (1982–86) and deputy editor of the *New Statesman* (1978–82). She has written widely on sustainable development, public health policy, public involvement and democratic dialogue, gender and equality.

Malcolm Dean has been a journalist for 46 years – 38 of them on *The Guardian* – climbing through the ranks as roving reporter, social affairs leader writer, social policy editor and from the mid-1980s, assistant editor. He set up and ran for most of its first 20 years *The Guardian*'s weekly Society section, which specialises in social policy, as well as writing daily editorials. He wrote the layperson's guide to the 24 research projects of the Economic and Social Research Council's (ESRC's) Growing Older programme; chaired a Joseph Rowntree Foundation commission on older people; and served on the Chief Medical Officer's advisory group on the regulation of doctors. He retired from *The Guardian* in 2006 and took up a fellowship at Nuffield College, Oxford, where he is writing a book on the media's influence on social policy.

Baroness Julia Neuberger DBE was educated at Newnham College, Cambridge, and Leo Baeck College, London. She became a rabbi in 1977, and served the South London Liberal Synagogue for 12 years, before going to The King's Fund Institute as a visiting fellow. She was at Harvard Medical School in 1991–92, Chair of Camden & Islington Community Health Services NHS Trust from 1993 until 1997 and then Chief Executive of The King's Fund, an independent health charity, until 2004. She has been a member of the Committee on Standards in Public Life, the Medical Research Council (MRC) and the General

Medical Council, and a trustee of the Runnymede Trust and the Imperial War Museum (until 2006). She was also a trustee of the British Council, and remains a trustee of Jewish Care and of the Booker Prize Foundation as well as a founding trustee of the Walter and Liesel Schwab Charitable Trust, in memory of her parents, and of New Philanthropy Capital, a charity that assesses the outcomes of charities' work. Until recently she chaired the independent Commission on the Future of Volunteering, she is President of Liberal Judaism, and last year she was appointed the Prime Minister's Champion for Volunteering. She is now the new Chair of the Responsible Gambling Strategy Board and has also just been appointed Chair of the One Housing Group.

She is the author of several books on Judaism, women, healthcare ethics and on caring for dying people. Her latest book, *Not dead yet: A manifesto for old age*, was published by HarperCollins in May 2008.

She was created a Life Peer in June 2004 (Liberal Democrat) and was Bloomberg Professor of Divinity at Harvard University for the spring semester of 2006.

Thomas Scharf is Professor of Social Gerontology and Director of the Centre for Social Gerontology at Keele University. His research explores a range of issues concerned with the social policy of ageing, with a particular emphasis on the themes of poverty and social exclusion in later life. In recent years he has developed a programme of work that addresses the experiences of older people who live in contrasting environments, including urban and rural settings and purpose-built retirement communities. His most recent book is *Critical perspectives on ageing societies* (2007, The Policy Press; co-edited with Miriam Bernard).

Alan Walker is Professor of Social Policy and Social Gerontology at the University of Sheffield, UK. He has been researching and writing on aspects of ageing and social policy for over 30 years. He is currently Director of the New Dynamics of Ageing programme (www.newdynamics.group.shef.ac.uk/) funded by the Arts & Humanities Research Council (AHRC), Biotechnology and Biological Sciences Research Council (BBSRC), Engineering and Physical Sciences Research Council (EPSRC), ESRC and MRC, and of the European Research Area in Ageing (www.shef.ac.uk/era-age/). Previously he directed the UK Growing Older programme (www.shef.ac.uk/uni/projects/gop/index.htm) and the European Forum on Population Ageing (www.shef.ac.uk/ageingresearch). He also chaired the European Observatory on Ageing and Older People.

He has published more than 20 books, 200 reports and 300 scientific papers. Recent books include *Growing older: Quality of life in older age* (2004), *Growing older in Europe* (2004) and *Understanding quality of life in old age* (2005), all published by McGraw Hill and *Quality of life in old age* (2007), published by Springer. In 2007 he was given Lifetime Achievement Awards by both the Social Policy Association and the British Society of Gerontology.

Acknowledgements

This book is dedicated to Help the Aged and its work for older people over its lifetime, from 1961 to 2009.

In particular we would like to thank Gill Rowley and Phil Rossall from the charity for their devoted attention and care in helping us to prepare the typescript.

ONE

How social age trumped social class?

Malcolm Dean

As New Year's Day dawned in 2009 there was a very special 100th anniversary. No, not another centenarian qualifying for a Queen's 'telegram', but the 100th anniversary of the start of British state pensions, introduced by Lloyd George's Liberal government on 1 January 1909. Grateful recipients were reported to have cried 'God bless the Lord George' as they collected the first of their weekly five shillings (25p, or about £20 in today's money).[1] For financial reasons the Treasury had insisted that it should not start before people were aged 70, and there should be strict means tests. So nothing unfamiliar there. But there were also 'character' tests, and among the ineligible were the unemployed, alcoholics, people who had been in prison in the last 10 years or those with incomes of over 12 shillings a week. Even so, about 500,000 people were eligible for the new benefit – 40 per cent of the 70-plus age group.[2]

Life expectancy at birth in those days was about 48 for men and 52 for women, but that was because of the phenomenally high infant and child mortality rates. In 1900 over one-third of all deaths were in the under-fives and barely more than 10 per cent in the over-75s.[3] Those who survived childhood had a reasonable chance of reaching 70 – the Bible's benchmark for the end of life, three score years and ten – and could expect to live for a further nine years.

According to the Office for National Statistics (ONS) the number of centenarians in this 100-year period began increasing slowly in the first 50 years, from 100 to 270, but has since spouted with enormous energy to about 12,000 in 2009.[4] The government's Actuary Department's projections for further growth are even more startling: by 2029 a fourfold increase to 48,000; by 2036 an eightfold increase to 96,000; and by 2046 a sixteenfold increase to 192,000. Equally startling is the projection for the babies born in 2009: one in four can expect to live to 100. Lower down the age cohorts the proportion of people over 65 is expected to grow by 60 per cent in the next 25 years, six times the rate of the general population rise. And in 2008 the ONS announced another demographic milestone: for the first time the number of pensioners in the UK (nearly 12 million) exceeded the number of under-16s.

There is nothing new about historic seismic population shifts. But previous shifts have normally been prompted by unpredictable events such as famine, plague or war. What *is* new is that this latest shift can be – and has been – anticipated. There has been a stream of predictions for well over a decade for a government ready to act. According to Professor Tom Kirkwood, Britain's first Professor of Biological Gerontology, who delivered the BBC Reith lectures in 2001, Britain has been adding two years to life every decade for 200 years: as he put it in his friendly, colloquial way, a long-running offer of an extra 20 per cent every day.[5] The early gains introduced by sanitation and piped water in the 19th century dramatically slashed infectious diseases and then vaccination and antibiotics in the 20th century extended the process. The ever-rising upward curve of life expectancy was meant to level out after that – as even a United Nations (UN) specialist panel as late as 1990 was forecasting – but it has not.[6] In Kirkwood's words, our bodies are not programmed for death, but for survival. There is not some unavoidable sell-by date or internal ticking clock. Ageing comes about through the gradual build-up of unrepaired faults in the cells and tissues of our bodies. It is a complicated process with multiple causes. But if we can discover the nature of the faults, we can slow their accumulation. Science has already made astonishing advances in understanding the basic chemistry of life – in genetics and genome research, in manipulating cells both inside the body and out of it – that should allow us a much greater understanding of the ageing process and open up new opportunities in forthcoming decades to make life more comfortable for older people.

One of the contributors to this book, Professor Alan Walker, was Director of the Economic and Social Research Council's (ESRC's) Growing Older programme that began in 1998 – the largest social science programme on ageing mounted in the UK. It had a budget of £3.5 million and 94 researchers, working on 24 projects, and it concluded in 2003. Although the profound changes that an ageing society signalled were already recognised in Whitehall, this issue was not being debated more widely in the UK. Instead, as Professor Walker observed at the time, the vacuum was filled by a demography of despair from the media, which 'portrayed population ageing not as a triumph for civilisation, but something closer to an apocalypse'.[7]

The media still prefer the negative to the positive, and, as Kirkwood noted, there are still a lot of negative elements in ageing. The ESRC looked at several of them, including the first national study of loneliness for 50 years, the first representative study of quality of life, a devastating examination of the exclusion of older people in deprived areas. Now Professor Walker is a director of an even bigger programme: a £12.5 million five-year interdisciplinary programme on the New Dynamics of Ageing, involving all four research councils – medicine, engineering, biotechnology and social science – that might make the scientific breakthroughs for which Kirkwood is hoping.

The cumulative losses of old age

> 'It's terrible at first. You get used to hanging around after six years but it's terrible at first. The highlight is going up to the post office! You've got nothing to do because you can't.... You lose pride in yourself, in your appearance. At first my wife had to remind me to have a shave and get dressed. I used to say "What's the point?". Especially in winter. You can't sit out like in summer. I absolutely dread winter.' (Older person made redundant between the age of 50 and 65, taken from *Winning the generation game*, 2000, published by the Performance and Innovation Unit)

The book you are reading concentrates on loss. It acknowledges that there have been large advances in the standard of living of many pensioners, and it accepts that the current generation of retired people – particularly pre-recession – were the most affluent in British history. In terms of income, 18 per cent of retired couples are now part of the richest fifth of the population.[8] In terms of wealth, the distribution is even starker: 85 per cent of the country's wealth is in the hands of the over-50s.[9] Three quarters of those aged 60–70 own their own home, as do 60 per cent of those over 70. People's net financial wealth (excluding housing and pension pots) increases with age to reach a peak in the mid-60s before starting to decline. One survey by the Sainsbury Bank, which caught media attention in 2003, suggested that six out of ten people over 50 were already – or intending – to take part in a new form of SKIing – Spending the Kids' Inheritance. No doubt the recession, a 37 per cent fall in equities, a 20 per cent decline in house prices and a precipitous drop in savings rates (from 5.2 to 0.5 per cent) will have helped circumscribe some of these plans. But it also seems clear that the survey could not have included many pensioners when 70 per cent of them rely on welfare benefits and pensions for at least half their income.[10]

Yet even at the bottom end there has been progress. Thirty-five years ago half the people living below the poverty line (60 per cent below the median national income) comprised pensioners. Today that proportion has been halved to a quarter.[11] In 1997 a new Labour government inherited 2.9 million pensioners living below the poverty line. This number was reduced to 2.5 million (before housing costs) and 2 million (after housing costs). This is still a huge number for one of the richest countries in the world with more income per head using purchasing power parity than France, Germany and Italy.

> 'I go round the supermarket where the stuff is reduced and buy it. You don't eat what you want to eat, you eat what's been reduced...' (Older person, taken from *Winning the generation game*, 2000, published by the Performance and Innovation Unit)

What is worse, in the latest statistics both the absolute number and the proportion of pensioners in poverty began to rise again in 2006/7.[12] This study does not stop at income, however. It looks at health, housing, environment, employment and quality of life. In each of these fields not only do gross inequalities remain but in many they are also actually widening. For a shockingly high number of pensioners, growing older is a journey of loss: loss of work, income, health, well-being, status, social networks and companions. Diseases associated with growing older multiply with the dramatic ageing of the population and years spent in ill health or with disability lengthen. Yet the response of communities and care systems is often inadequate and ageism abounds.

The age-old problem of ageism

Let us begin with ageism, which affects not just poor pensioners but older people across the board. According to Pat Thane, London University professor and author of many studies of ageing, there has never been a golden age for being old in Britain. In a lecture at King's College, London in 2004, in memory of David Hobman, a former director of Age Concern, she reported: 'I am frequently asked, "When did we stop respecting older people like we used to?" My response is that there was never a time in our culture when older people have been respected simply for being old.' She also doubted whether families were more supportive of older people in the past than they are now.

Before the 20th century older people were less likely than now to have families to support them. Only about one-third of people in their

60s had surviving children in the early 19th century because of high death rates. And many of those who did would have lost touch with them through the hundreds of thousands who migrated for a better life in Australia, Canada, New Zealand and South Africa, or moved to work in another part of Britain to which there was poor transport.[13] Pat Thane pointed back to as long ago as 1834, the year when the Royal Commission on the Poor Laws noted how civilised nations and even savages recognised a duty of support for older parents, but added: 'We believe that Britain is the only European nation where it [the duty] is neglected.'

An opinion poll taken of older people to coincide with the merger in April 2009 of the two biggest charities supporting them, Age Concern and Help the Aged, found them in no doubt about the ageism in our current society: 60 per cent believed age discrimination still existed in everyday life; 60 per cent that it still existed in the workplace; and 68 per cent that politicians still saw older people as a low priority.[14] Six years earlier, in July 2003, the government produced a consultative document on ageism in which Patricia Hewitt, the Cabinet minister responsible for it, suggested that ageism was not taken as seriously as racism in our society for two reasons: first, because it was not rooted in hostility or ill feeling; and, second, because as everyone faced growing older, most people became resigned to it.[15] There is some truth in both assertions, but what they ignored was the lessons learned from fighting racism.

There are three forms of discrimination, not one: overt and intentional; disguised but deliberate; unintentional but adverse. It is the last two categories that are the most difficult to eliminate and that pose the greatest threat.

In October 2006, Tessa Harding MBE, who joined Help the Aged in 1996, gave a moving farewell lecture that I chaired. Its theme was the long and winding road towards dignity and equality in old age.[16] Prior to her joining the charity she had worked alongside disabled people who were busy shaping the disability movement, which rejected the patronising and paternalistic attitudes of the day. She spoke of how 'age discrimination' was hardly on the agenda in the UK in 1996; of the lack of acknowledgement of older people as full and equal citizens; of the 'benign' paternalism that echoed an earlier age when women were unable to get a mortgage in their own name before women's rights. Let me quote the lecture's powerful opening paragraph, which still has resonance today:

I want to suggest that we have hardly yet begun to grasp the scale and impact of age discrimination on our society. We expect older people to be treated unequally and to be treated worse than their young counterparts. That is how policies are constructed, how services are shaped and how the environment is arranged. Age discrimination is so integral to our thinking, so much part of the accepted way of doing things and so taken for granted in how we see and interpret the world around us, that our judgement is coloured, our perceptions affected and our expectations shaped, whatever age we are.

It certainly resonated with me, having heard frequent references to, for example, the systematic way in which hard-pressed social services departments routinely robbed older people's budgets to boost children's services over the decades. Or take the Disability Living Allowance, which is intended to meet the additional costs associated with having an impairment irrespective of income – but you are only eligible to apply if you become disabled under the age of 65. If you are 65 or over when you become disabled, you may only apply for Attendance Allowance, which takes longer to qualify for, is less generous and does not include a sum to meet mobility costs.

The most radical solution to changing attitudes was proposed by Michael Young, Britain's greatest social entrepreneur of the last century, who created The Open University, the Consumers' Association and the School for Social Entrepreneurs, among 57 other social enterprises. In 1990 in a leading lecture to the British Association he proposed the abolition of age as a governing criterion and the redistribution of leisure, education and work over the lifespan. Given that, arguably, the greatest achievement of the 20th century was the reduction of biological ageing, it was time for the 21st century to concentrate on the injuries of social ageing. Society was trying to slot people into a fixed chronology even though ageing did not occur at a uniform rate – chronological age could not be a proxy for capacity and competence. Social age had replaced social class as a principle behind collective organisation. Career timetables were drawn up to indicate what rank people should have reached at a particular age. If you got off the train, you frequently could not get on again. The compulsory registration of births dated back only to 1836, yet age standardisation was deeply embedded in law and custom. Birthdays were no longer private but had to be repeatedly declared to show entitlement. His solution was an end to compulsory retirement and the extension of the Data Protection

Act to dates of birth. We have not got either yet, but we could get the first shortly.

Progress

There has been progress. We now have a body to police age discrimination and to promote age equality in public services that began on 1 October 2007: the Equality and Human Rights Commission (EHRC). The EHRC brought together three former commissions dealing with race, gender and disability and added three other fields of protection: age, sexual orientation and belief (religion). But one of the most glaring anomalies, until the new Equality Bill, published in 2009, becomes law, is that currently the EHRC, set up to promote equality, has unequal powers with respect to the people it is meant to be protecting. In five of the fields requiring protection the EHRC can intercede not just in the field of employment but also against discrimination in the provision of goods, facilities and services. With respect to older people, however, it is currently restricted to discrimination in employment. A pub landlord could refuse you a drink on the grounds of age without any legal recourse. Belatedly, ministers have finally conceded that all six streams under its umbrella should have equal protection.

In October 2006 the government also implemented a new law banning age discrimination in employment and vocational training.

> 'What has amazed me most is my own decline in self-worth. I never thought someone with my energy and optimism could ever be daunted. If unemployment can get someone of my temperament down, it can negatively affect anyone.' (Older person made redundant between the age of 50 and 65, taken from *Winning the generation game*, 2000, published by the Performance and Innovation Unit)

The 2006 law requires all employers to review their employment practices – recruitment, promotion, training, pay, pensions, redundancy and retirement – to ensure they are based on skills and competences, not age. Over 2,000 tribunal claims were lodged in the first year of the Act's implementation. It was aimed particularly at the 50–65 age group, which had suffered a huge drop in male employment: from 90 per cent in the early 1970s to 65 per cent in the mid-1990s, with only a third in employment in their 64th year. Of the 2.5 million not in work in this group, 1.5 million had been given involuntary redundancy. Even employers, or at least the enlightened ones that joined the Employers'

Forum on Age, openly admitted that ageism was endemic in the workplace. They estimated that ageism was costing the economy, in lost tax and benefits, £30 billion a year.

Unfortunately the regulations in the Act were marred by the introduction of a 'default' retirement age, which meant that people could still be retired against their will when they reached the age of 65. As Tessa Harding noted: 'We may not have had legislation against age discrimination before, but neither, until now, have we had legislation which expressly permits it.'

A ministerial U-turn

The long-drawn-out compulsory retirement saga began with a European Union (EU) directive requiring member states to end compulsory retirement ages. Initially the government signalled that it would be robust in introducing this directive, and in 2003 it released age discrimination proposals under which workers would have been allowed to work until 70, if they wished. This would still have breached the principle, but worse was to come. Under pressure from the Confederation of British Industry (CBI), which was insisting that a statutory retirement age of 65 was an essential management tool, ministers made a U-turn and took the CBI position. The issue has still to be decided by the High Court. The British judges asked the European Court of Justice for guidance on EU law, which ruled earlier in 2009 that the UK's approach could be legal if there was legitimate employment or social policy backing. The issue is now back with the High Court, where the government will have to show a clear and unequivocal public interest behind the move. Many well-informed observers believe this will be difficult, but should the government win, opposition MPs as well as peers are planning to attach an amendment to the Equality Bill. Similar retirement laws, banning a mandatory retirement age, were introduced in the US in 1967, in New South Wales in 1977, in Ireland in 1998 and in Denmark in 2004.

What the government seems to be ignoring is the forecast from the UK Commission for Employment and Skills that the country will need to find 13.5 million more workers – from a combination of retirements and new technological demands – between 2007 and 2017, when only 7 million young people are expected to leave school and university.[17] Ministers are also ignoring what enlightened firms in the private sector along with some local councils are doing: Nationwide's decision in 2005 to let staff work to 75; the Co-operative Group, which has got rid of a set retirement age altogether; and B&Q, which has for some years been purposefully recruiting over-50s – now more than 25 per cent of its 34,000-strong workforce – because of their enthusiasm for the work, much lower absenteeism and their greater rapport with customers.

The ultimate irony is that a government which continues to preach the need for its workforce to work longer – and even passed a Pension Act that progressively extends retirement age to 68 by 2046 – is still trapped in 20th-century attitudes in terms of helping older people to work longer now if they so wish. Until the recession the numbers of workers in the 50–65 age cohort and post-65 were climbing – from 65 per cent in the 1990s to 72 per cent by the end of 2008 for the first group, and from 9 to 11 per cent for the second.[18] But, as happened in the last recession, the 50–65 age group has been the hardest hit by the present recession.

It is worth remembering in the wake of the big battles over legislation the smaller indirect discriminations which cumulatively can cause serious losses in older people's lives: the loss of post offices, smaller corner shops, newsagents, local pubs, regular buses, public toilets – all of which have been drastically reduced in the past two decades. The current recession can only make this situation worse. And then there is the lack of seats in supermarkets, at bus stops and in some public squares and parks.

Society's construct of ageing

In her fascinating chapter (Five) in this book, Baroness Julia Neuberger, author of the recently published book *Not dead yet*, with its spirited 10-point manifesto,[19] looks at the perceptions of ageing today, explores the causes of current prejudices and explains why it matters and what we can do about it. She notes that some of the best voluntary organisations still apply age bans on volunteers and calls to account professionals with their skewed view of what successful ageing consists of: physical functioning, adaptability, coping and self-esteem, according to two academics who carried out a large literature review. The professionals had left out a long list of definitions that older people themselves had identified, including enjoyment of food, a sense of purpose, physical appearance, a sense of humour, contributions to life, financial security and a sense of spirituality.

Like others, Baroness Neuberger despairs at how such a large and diverse number of people with a 40-year-plus age span – from 60 to over 100 – are telescoped into one stereotype. She goes on: 'Nor can we rely on this phenomenon simply working itself out, as people realise its absurdity. All the experience of other forms of discrimination suggests that does not work, and that society has to set itself goals to root out age discrimination.'

Among the causes of prejudices, she includes the remarkably scant contact between different age groups; fear of death and the degree to which older people can be a constant and uncomfortable reminder of its inevitability; fear of the demand on resources of an ageing population; and the difficulty which modern societies face in placing a value on people who no longer make an economic contribution. If old age 'merely reminds us of our mortality, of loss, of lack of value, of lack of productivity, of pointlessness, it is all too easy to see how prejudice against these parasites on society can grow'. What do we do about this? Her answer is the need for a more politically proactive and assertive grey power movement, ready to express its exasperation: 'We need the voices of anger that we hear clearly but all too rarely, about the injustices and the lack of respect – and therefore self-respect – that goes with them.'

The three chapters that follow on income, health and housing (Chapters Two, Three and Four) document the widening inequalities in each of these fields. The authors are all respected experts on these issues. Thomas Scharf, Director of the Centre for Social Gerontology at Keele University, was the leader of the devastating study on life in three of the most deprived wards in the ESRC's Growing Older programme. Anna Coote is a former director of Health Policy at The King's Fund and then led the Healthcare Commission's work on engaging patients and the public. Sue Adams is Director of Care & Repair England, which was set up in 1986 to improve the housing and living conditions of older people.

Following Baroness Neuberger's reflections (Chapter Five) on what it means to be old, in Chapter Six Bryan Appleyard, author and distinguished *Sunday Times* journalist, answers her call for more passion in an angry essay on quality of life that rightly takes his trade – and mine – to task for its obsession with youth and the stereotyping of age. He could also have mentioned the media's distorted values. Compare two grisly deaths from abuse and how they were treated. Victoria Climbié, aged 8, died in 2000 from severe abuse, neglect and multiple injuries – including burns and scalds – inflicted by her great aunt who had brought her to England from Sierra Leone. Her death generated massive media coverage, including 303 news and feature stories and 237 in the nationals. One year later, Margaret Panting, aged 78, died from similar severe abuse, neglect and multiple injuries – burns and razor cuts – within five weeks of being moved from sheltered accommodation to her son-in-law's house. Her death just generated five news stories, only two of them in the nationals.

Alan Walker, Professor of Social Policy and Social Gerontology at Sheffield University, wrote the penultimate chapter in this book, listing the multiple causes that combine to produce cumulative negative outcomes in old age. He also points to the origins of the basic state pension and Beveridge's belief that it should provide only a first tier on which supplements should be built. This has been exacerbated by huge disparities in occupational and personal pensions, along with the unfair tax breaks they generate for the better-off. And then there was Britain's failure to establish the right baseline for pensions, unlike Sweden, which followed the Beveridge principle but rejected Anglo-Saxon minimalism and went for generous provision to create a more equal citizenship.

The final chapter in this book was written by my co-editor, Paul Cann, former Director of Policy, Research and International Development at Help the Aged and now Chief Executive of Age Concern Oxfordshire. He sets out in lucid prose a coherent strategy for the future from cash, through rights and options, better use of technology, earlier preventive work, a clearer focus on tackling isolation and improving well-being, along with the expansion of the LinkAge Plus pilots – which demonstrated how services can be integrated – into a nationwide programme. Here is a package that could drastically reduce the current losses that older people suffer and make immeasurable improvements to their lives.

Ever-widening inequality gaps

Just as this book was being written, Richard Wilkinson and Kate Pickett produced their devastating comparisons of 22 developed states in *The spirit level*, which has been widely covered in the media.[20] The UK, where the income of someone in the top fifth of all incomes receives seven times as much on average as someone in the bottom fifth, was up at the top of the inequality league. Only Portugal (eight times as much) and the US (eight-and-a-half times as much) were more unequal. Japan and Finland, the most equal with only half as much inequality, enjoy much healthier populations, longer lives and more trust between people. Getting richer used to make countries healthier and happier, but this no longer happens in states at the top of the inequality league.

Not only have the measures of well-being and happiness ceased to rise with economic growth but, as these affluent but unequal societies have grown richer, so has there been a rise in rates of anxiety, depression and premature death across all income groups, albeit to a diminishing extent. And so has the extent of social problems expanded: crime, drugs, obesity and poorer mental health. The authors suggest that inequality increases stress and anxiety about status. Even most of the better-off know people better off than themselves and are aware of people falling down the social ladder. The authors quote a nationwide survey of North Americans that found them 'deeply ambivalent about wealth and material gain', with a large majority wanting to 'move away from greed and excess toward a way of life more centred on values, community and family'. Something similar could be happening in the UK after the collapse of banks, the stock market and house prices that began in the autumn of 2007. Even the most right-wing papers – the *Daily Mail* and *Daily Telegraph* – have been condemning the get-rich society that they once used to fulsomely propagate. Polls over the past three decades have shown a large majority in the UK wanting a fairer Britain, but giving less support for using taxation to achieve this. The exposure of the gross bonuses and pension pots paid to city bosses could well have changed this. Sir Fred Goodwin – 'Fred the Shred' in tabloid-speak – who received a £16 million pension pot courtesy of the directors of the Royal Bank of Scotland, was the most extreme example. The bank he had been head of recorded the largest loss in British corporate history (£24 million) and had to be bailed out by the government (ie, taxpayers).

It is worth remembering just how unequal the UK became during the 18 years of Conservative administration (1979–97), most of it generated in the 1980s. Both child and pensioner poverty accelerated at an alarming rate: child poverty more than doubling after housing costs (from one in seven to one in three children below the poverty line), while pensioner poverty increased even faster, tripling the proportions from 13 to 41 per cent below the poverty line.[21] And they were not the only ones to suffer.

As the team of London School of Economics and Political Science (LSE) academics who monitored the first 10 years of the Labour government (1997–2007) documented, Tony Blair inherited levels of poverty and inequality unprecedented in post-war (1945) history,[22] and as an earlier version of that book noted in 2005:

> Unlike every other post-war decade, in which the gains of economic growth were shared across income groups, growth in the 1980s benefited the richest most and the poorest least. Indeed, on one measure, the incomes of the

very poorest were lower in real terms in 1994/5 than they
had been in 1979.

No European country suffered such a widening of inequality, the gap
between the rich and poor doubling. In 1979 the post-tax income of
the top tenth of the population was five times as much as the bottom
tenth; by 1997 that proportion doubled to 10 times as much.[23] This
was achieved by slashing top-rate income tax from 80 to 40 per cent
and some 20 different squeezes on benefits, the most serious of which
for pensioners was to end the pension link with earnings from 1979.
Thanks to occupational and personal pensions, the overall income of
pensioners increased at a faster rate than average earnings. But those
dependent on the state pension fell back. The inequality gap between
pensioners got even wider, with the incomes of the richest fifth rising
three times faster (by 90 per cent) than the poorest fifth (by 30 per
cent) over the 18 years of Conservative government.[24]

Labour made a public pledge during the 1997 General Election that
it would not increase top-rate tax above the existing 40 per cent – it
believed it had lost the 1992 election with a manifesto that had included
tax rises. Once in office it maintained this position – Peter Mandelson
famously saying 'We are intensely relaxed about people getting filthy
rich' – until the record rise in government debt forced the Chancellor
to announce a 50 per cent rate in his 2009 Budget, to begin in April
2010. Two key anti-poverty measures by Labour were the launch of
the Social Exclusion Unit in its first year and in its second the pledge
to abolish child poverty within a generation. There was no matching
ambition with respect to pensions.

Pensions

Labour inherited a pension system in 1997 which was already shifting
in three important ways:

- overall from public towards private provision
- within the public sector, from an income guaranteed by the
  contributions of state pension towards one guaranteed through
  means-testing
- within the private sector, from one where the risk was shared to
  one where the risk was individualised.[25]

In 2002 Labour set up the Turner Commission, ostensibly to focus on
pension savings, but it widened its brief to look at the whole system,

exposing critical shortcomings: the average employer/employee contribution to occupational schemes had fallen from 19 to 9 per cent of salary; only 18 million out of 34 million people of working age in the UK were contributing either directly or through a partner to a private pension; some 12 million who were making contributions were not saving enough and faced cuts of up to 30 per cent in current retirement incomes.

Where once workers' retirement was seen as a tripartite responsibility shared by the government, employer and employee, the first two had shed large parts of their risk, loading more weight on to employees – all this when Britain's state pension was already one of the least generous in the developed world, providing the average (male) retired worker with 31 per cent of average earnings compared with 39 per cent in the US, 43 per cent in Germany, 45 per cent in Canada, 53 per cent in France, 62 per cent in Sweden, 68 per cent in Italy, 80 per cent in Denmark, 81 per cent in Spain and 88 per cent in the Netherlands. An OECD (Organisation for Economic Co-operation and Development) report in 2009 placed Britain 30th (bottom) in its pension league of 30 member states, where men's pensions average 59 per cent.[26]

Ironically, in a country that is proud of not being a welfare state, the US has a much more stable pension system than the UK, which has had multiple reforms in the past four decades. The US replacement ratio – the 39 per cent proportion of average earnings – is sufficient to ensure the sharp elbows of the middle class as well as low-income families will fight to defend it. So successful and popular is the system that not even successive Republican administrations have been able to cut it.

Like Beveridge 67 years before him, Turner's report caught a popular tide. His interim report in 2004 put forward three tough options to save the system: more savings, higher tax and a longer working life. His final report in 2005 sensibly set out a combination of all three. It helped achieve a considerable consensus with the two Pensions Acts (2007 and 2008) that followed, widening eligibility particularly for women, increasing savings, extending retirement over time to the age of 68, along with provisions to restore the earnings link. But the two Acts have done little for existing pensioners. According to the Institute for Fiscal Studies, pensioner poverty is likely to remain at current levels – 2.5 million – despite the reform measures,[27] while the bill for unclaimed means-tested benefits – Pension Credit, Council Tax Benefit and Housing Benefit – loses pensioners up to £5 billion a year.[28]

In Chapter Two, Thomas Scharf rightly questions why the government committed itself – with specific targets – to abolishing child poverty, but is only ready to make reductions of pensioner poverty an aspiration. It has even dropped its Pension Credit take-up target. Scharf points to the large numbers of single-pensioner householders, particularly single-female households, who are clustered in the bottom two-fifths of income distribution. These are people with a heightened risk of living in persistent poverty. He goes on:

> In this respect, there is a crucial difference between the poverty experienced by children and young people and that of older people: children born into poverty have a range of potential opportunities to escape their financial hardship – through education, training, employment, household formation or inheritance. Older people who enter retirement on a low income have very few opportunities to improve their financial circumstances. This is why the state has to assume a crucial role in relation to alleviating the poverty experienced by older people.

Scharf led one of the research teams in the ESRC Growing Older programme, which produced a devastating report of life in three of the most deprived wards in the country – one each from Manchester, Liverpool and London. He draws on his interview with a single female pensioner in Liverpool, Flora Peters, to give readers an insight into the difficulties that poor pensioners face. Read it and see a human face behind the welter of statistics.

Grim losses in health

Of all the elements of life, none offers more examples of loss than health. The list is frightening – partial loss of sight, loss of hearing, loss of physical strength – before listing conditions even more closely associated with ageing, such as osteoporosis, hip fractures, osteoarthritis, stroke, incontinence, dementia and depression. Welcome though the lengthening of life expectancy has been, the postponement of the onset of ill health and disability has not been able to maintain the same pace. Thus, while life expectancy has lengthened, so have the number of years of ill health and disability. In 2006 a man aged 65 could expect a further 16.9 years of life – 10.1 years free of disability but 6.8 years with at least one disability. A woman aged 65 could expect 19.7 years with 10.6 years free of disability but 9.1 years with at least one disability.[29] And it is even worse for the poorest older people, who are five times more likely than the richest to have poor health, five times more likely to have difficulty walking and up to four times more likely to suffer severe joint pain.[30]

Now, as Baroness Neuberger notes in Chapter Five (and Anna Coote examines in much more detail in Chapter Three), these statistics can cause much despair. There are many things that can be done with the onset of chronic conditions or disabilities, and there is even more that can be done in earlier life to prevent them. As Sir Michael Marmot, the epidemiologist and world-renowned expert on health inequalities said in the 2002 English Longitudinal Study of Ageing (ELSA), published in 2004:

> Middle age is no paradise; old age is no hell. This does not mean that middle-aged people are immune to declines in function. Surprisingly, 43 per cent of respondents in their 50s reported some difficulty with mobility. Similarly, difficulties with independent living increase with age. This does not mean that all older people have difficulty: 58 per cent of respondents in their 80s and beyond have no difficulties with basic activities of daily life. The challenge for the future is to understand what leads some 80-year-olds to high levels of functioning and some 50-year-olds already to show signs of decline.[31]

One reason why some people develop a chronic illness before others is poverty. As Anna Coote documents in Chapter Three, poor people's health starts to decline earlier than that of better-off people, and then gets worse more rapidly. She quotes one study of men aged between 45 and 65 that found that the level of incapacity experienced by men in the lowest income class by their mid-50s was not reached by men in the top income class until their mid-60s.[32]

Sir Michael, who is chair of the World Health Organization's (WHO) Commission on Social Determinants of Health, revealed in August 2008 an astounding Scottish statistic on inequality of health discovered by his large team of researchers: a boy in the deprived district of Calton, Glasgow, can expect to live 28 years less than a boy brought up in affluent Lenzie, just a few miles away. The media was used to ministers using the story of a London Tube journey east from affluent Westminster, where each of the seven stops on the Jubilee line to less affluent Canning Town marked a community with a one-year drop in life expectancy: a seven-year gap by the end. But a gap of 28 years – nobody had heard that before. The statistic ensured blanket coverage in the British press. The Calton boy's 54 years of life expectancy is eight years less than the average Indian's. Three months later Alan Johnson, Health Secretary, asked Sir Michael to lead a major government review of health inequalities in England.

Social care: still the Cinderella

Health specialists have warned for years that the National Health Service (NHS) alone cannot cure the nation's sickness and disabilities. What is needed is better housing, cleaner environments, wider opportunities for sport and exercise, more regulation of fast food outlets and better social care. I chaired a Joseph Rowntree Foundation commission on 'That bit of help' for older people that reported in 2006.[33] Three decades previously it had been much easier for older people to find a home help to carry out minor tasks. Now, the number of hours of help provided in people's homes has doubled, but the number helped has fallen by 60 per cent. What began as a low-level support service has become a high-dependency service to keep people out of residential care. While this is an admirable goal, we concluded that a little bit more help upstream could help delay some of the high-dependency help needed downstream.

Other problems with the current social care system include unequal charges, unacceptable variations in standards and an unjust approach to different diseases (such as free healthcare for cancer and coronary patients but means-tested care for those suffering from Alzheimer's or Parkinson's). Earlier in 2009 the Commission for Social Care Inspection (CSCI)[34] warned that the ever-tightening eligibility rules for council funding of social care would generate an increasingly sharp divide between those who qualified to get some help and those who failed.

Like the NHS, social care involves more than a million workers, but that is where the comparisons stop. Unlike the NHS, two-thirds of the social care workforce is in the voluntary or private sector. Unlike the NHS, the 1.3 million employees are mostly unqualified and distributed across 26,000 employers. Unlike that of the NHS, the social care budget did not double in seven years. Yet the systems are umbilically linked. Many of the people in the NHS's biggest client group – the 17 million suffering from a chronic disease – also have social care needs. There have been Green Papers, and pilots, and partnerships and some integration between health and social services, but at the time of writing, all we are offered is another Green Paper. We need much more, as Alan Johnson conceded at the London conference in April 2009 marking the merger of Age Concern and Help the Aged: 'We need to approach the reform of social care with the same urgency and determination and, above all, imagination, of those who created the post-war consensus on welfare reform.' He promised that the Green Paper would be more than a list of funding options, that it would involve 'a vision for a kind of care system that will match and exceed the expectations of older people'.[35]

Of course, it should have been done years ago – long before the recession hit. It will cost money but it ought to be met. Sir Derek Wanless, who transformed the funding of the health service with his 2002 report, produced a 300-page report on social care for The King's Fund in 2006.[36] It won widespread support. Everyone in need would be entitled to an agreed level of free care, after which individuals' contributions would be matched by the state up to a defined level.

One further paradox of the shortcomings of social care is that without older people care would be in an even worse mess. According to a well-documented 2009 report from Grandparents Plus[37] there are 14 million grandparents, one in three of whom have a dependent child living with them and half with a living parent of their own. Two-thirds live within 10 miles of their grandchildren. In terms of childcare Grandparents Plus quotes an Institution of Education report[38] that found that grandparents provide 40 per cent of childcare for parents who are at work or studying and 70 per cent at other times. But many are also looking after their own disabled parents or partners too. The report noted:

> The traditional image of the sandwich generation woman (for it is still women who provide most of the care) is caring for children and parents, but she is increasingly likely to be managing three generational caring responsibilities, with the added complexity that a step-family may then bring. This multiplicity of roles (simultaneously as mother, carer, grandmother, step-grandmother) and circumstances requires the family to adapt and also means that the nuclear model becomes less and less relevant.

Housing and neighbourhoods

As Sue Adams notes in Chapter Four, there is no more visible symbol of wealth and status than a person's home. And there is no more obvious evidence of widening inequalities in Britain than comparing the state of affluent suburban residences with conditions in run-down inner-city housing estates. Of seven different dimensions of social exclusion identified by researchers for a social exclusion report in 2006, five of the seven affecting older people were connected to deprivation of place.[39]

Doubters should read Scharf's ESRC *Growing Older* report[40] from three of the most deprived wards in England: 70 per cent of older people were experiencing some form of social exclusion, with 40 per cent suffering multiple exclusions – they were not just poor, but socially isolated as a result of cuts in basic services, were fearful of crime in their neighbourhood and excluded from civic activities. Nearly half the people surveyed were poor – twice the national pensioner poverty rate. Almost half those in poverty had gone without buying clothes in the previous year, 15 per cent had occasionally gone without buying food and 14 per cent cut back on gas, electricity or telephone use. On a list of 26 items which 50 per cent of people believe to be basic amenities of daily life, 45 per cent were found unable to afford two (the definition of poverty) and 7 per cent unable to afford 11.[41] One-fifth of the older people were identified as socially isolated – lacking contact with children, relatives, friends or neighbours – and 16 per cent suffered from severe or very severe loneliness (scoring nine or more on an 11-item scale). Similarly, on civic activities, although 68 per cent of the older people in the survey voted at the previous general election and 66 per cent in the local election that followed, 24 per cent had not taken part in any of a list of 11 civic activities.

Of course, this was at the extreme end and the three-year study concluded in 2002. Progress has been made since then, but the 4,000 most deprived housing estates on which the Social Exclusion Unit report of 1998 was based are still a long way from transformation.[42] For the four million people who live on them, there is also the problem of the stigma attached to these estates and the degree to which it lingers on even after renovation.

The latest report[43] from the LSE team monitoring Labour's anti-poverty programmes suggests that in the 12 areas monitored, its poor neighbourhood renewal programmes did achieve over a 50 per cent reduction in environmental damage and a reduction in visible degradation, prompting a fall in the numbers of families wanting to opt out. But the author, Anne Power, expressed concern that such progress looked precarious because there was no commitment by the government to continue its area-based initiatives. What Labour did achieve was a major £30 billion-plus renovation of social rented housing in a 10-year drive to achieve the Decent Homes Standard introduced in 2000. As Sue Adams notes in Chapter Four, older people occupy 34 per cent of all social rented housing and would have gained significant housing improvements under this programme. Privately rented housing repairs did not keep pace with the progress in social housing renovations, and with the end of the Decent Homes target in 2008 is unlikely to catch up.

Successive governments have downgraded housing as a priority. This began under Margaret Thatcher but continued under Tony Blair. In the first eight years of the Blair government public expenditure on social housing was below the early 1990s, less than half the 1970s and two-thirds less than the 1960s.[44] A much-quoted Joseph Rowntree Foundation study in 2002 produced an astounding figure: the completion rate for public and private housing had reached its lowest point (outside the Second World War years) since 1924. The gap between demand and supply was widening by as much as 56,000 homes a year.[45] To his credit, when Gordon Brown took over at Number 10 in the summer of 2007, he did recognise the need for a vast increase in house construction, but then sub-prime mortgages in the US imploded and the recession that followed has squeezed all life out of the start of his expanded housing plan. The collapse of the housing market has led to a 72 per cent fall in the number of house starts in the year ending in March 2009, compared to the previous year, the lowest number once again since 1924.[46]

The politics of an ageing population

Finally, how strong a political hand does the older people's lobby hold? Will the growing numbers of post-Second World War baby boomers – 15 million retiring in the next 20 years – shift political attitudes? Some say they will not make a difference because they are a diverse group. But that ignores the findings of an Age Concern report in 2004,[47] which found growing numbers of older people (1.8 million) defining themselves as floating voters, many for the first time. It ignores the huge proportion of older voters who do vote – twice the proportion of the under-25s. It also ignores what happened in the run-up to the 2005 General Election when all three main parties competed in a Dutch auction to outbid each other in favours for older voters. In Labour's final budget in March, just weeks before the election, older people won by far the largest share: £800 million of the extra £2 billion on offer that was delivered. The Conservatives trumped that with a £1.3 billion offer to cut Council Tax bills by 50 per cent for households containing only over-65s, but did not get the opportunity to deliver. I am looking forward to hearing what bribes the next election will produce. My criteria will be how far the parties are ready to go with the Wanless model, how ready they are to reach a consensus and how quickly they are ready to implement it.

Notes

[1] Rupert Jones, *The Guardian*, 3 January 2009.

[2] Professor Pat Thane, letter to *Daily Telegraph*, 5 September 2008.

[3] Metz, D. and Underwood, M. (2005) *Older, richer, fitter: Identifying the customer needs of Britain's ageing population*, London: Age Concern.

[4] ONS, annual population estimates.

[5] Original lectures can be found on the BBC website (www.bbc.co.uk).

[6] Tom Kirkwood, essay in *The Observer*, 3 April 2005.

[7] Dean, M. (2003) *Growing older in the 21st century*, Swindon: ESRC. A summary of the 24 reports of the ESRC Growing Older programme for lay people.

[8] Metz, D. and Underwood, M. (2005) *Older, richer, fitter: Identifying the customer needs of Britain's ageing population*, London: Age Concern.

[9] Ibid.

[10] Ibid.

[11] Ibid.

[12] Hills, J., Sefton, T. and Stewart, K. (eds) (2009) *Towards a more equal society? Poverty, inequality and social policy since 1997*, Bristol: The Policy Press, p 171.

[13] Pat Thane lecture, 26 January 2004: 'The experience of ageing in Britain: the last 175 years.'

[14] Age Concern and Help the Aged (2009) *One voice: Shaping our ageing society*, London: Age Concern and Help the Aged. Launch publication for the merger between Age Concern and Help the Aged, 7 April 2009.

[15] Consultative document on ageing, Department of Trade, July 2003, introduced by Patricia Hewitt, Secretary of State.

[16] Later published as a pamphlet: Harding, T. (2006) *The long and winding road*, London: Help the Aged.

[17] UK Commission for Employment and Skills projections for 2007–17.

[18] Department for Work and Pensions (DWP) figures announced at One Voice conference (Age Concern and Help the Aged) in London, 7 April 2009, by Phil Yeoman, Head of Extending Working Life, DWP.

[19] Neuberger, J. (2008) *Not dead yet: A manifesto for old age*, London: HarperCollins.

[20] Wilkinson, R. and Pickett, K. (2009) *The spirit level: Why more equal societies almost always do better*, London: Allen Lane.

[21] Child poverty rates: see p 72, Table 4.1tr in DWP (2008) *Households Below Average Income: An analysis of the income distribution 1994/5–2006/7*, London: DWP. Pensioner poverty rates are on page 22 in Goodman, A., Myck, M. and Shephard, A. (2003) *Sharing in the nation's prosperity? Pensioner poverty in Britain*, IFS Commentary 93, London: Institute for Fiscal Studies, March.

[22] Hills, J., Sefton, T. and Stewart, K. (eds) (2009) *Towards a more equal society? Poverty, inequality and social policy since 1997*, Bristol: The Policy Press, p 2.

[23] Hills, J. and Stewart, K. (eds) (2005) *A more equal society? New Labour, poverty, inequality and exclusion*, Bristol: The Policy Press, p 1.

[24] Ibid, p 168.

[25] Hills, J., Sefton, T. and Stewart, K. (eds) (2009) *Towards a more equal society? Poverty, inequality and social policy since 1997*, Bristol: The Policy Press, p 162.

[26] OECD (Organisation for Economic Co-operation and Development) (2009) *Pensions at a glance 2009: Retirement-income systems in OECD countries* (http://ocde.p4.siteinternet.com/publications/doifiles/812009081P1T004.xls).

[27] Brewer, M., Browne, J., Emmerson, C., Goodman, A., Muriel, A. and Tetlow, G. (2007) *Pensioner poverty over the next decade: What role for tax and benefit reform?*, IFS Commentary 103, London: Institute for Fiscal Studies, July.

[28] Help the Aged estimates from DWP (2008) *Income-related benefits: Estimates of take-up in 2006/7*, London: DWP.

[29] 'Life expectancy at birth and at 65 by local areas in the United Kingdom, 2005–7', *Health Statistical Quarterly*, no 40, ONS, Winter 2008.

[30] Breeze, E. and Pearce, M. (2006) ELSA wave 2 launch presentation on health (the figures are calculated on the changes between waves 1 and 2). Available on Institute of Fiscal Studies website (www.ifs.org.uk/elsa).

[31] Marmot, M., Banks, J., Blundell, R., Lessof, C. and Nazroo, J. (eds) (2004) *Health, wealth and lifestyles of the older population in England: The 2002 English Longitudinal Study of Ageing*, London: Institute for Fiscal Studies.

[32] Graham, H. (2007) *Unequal lives: Health and socio-economic inequalities*, Milton Keynes: Open University Press, pp 156–7.

[33] Raynes, N., Clark, H. and Beecham, J. (eds) (2006) *Evidence submitted to the Older People's Inquiry into 'That bit of help'*, York: Joseph Rowntree Foundation.

[34] *The state of social care in England, 2006/7*, January 2008 and *Cutting the cake fairly*, October 2008, both by the Commission for Social Care Inspection.

[35] Alan Johnson, Secretary of State for Health, address to the One Voice conference (Age Concern and Help the Aged) in London, 7 April 2009, on the Department of Health website.

[36] Wanless Social Care Review (2006) *Securing good care for older people: Taking a long-term view*, The King's Fund.

[37] Grandparents Plus (2009) *Rethinking family life: Exploring the role of grandparents and the wider family*, 18 Victoria Park Square, London E2 9PF.

[38] *The Journal of Social Policy*, Cambridge University Press, February 2009 (Institute of Education press release, 10 February 2009).

[39] Barnes, M., Blom, A., Cox, K., Lessof, C. and Walker, A. (2006) *The social exclusion of older people: Evidence from the first wave of the English Longitudinal Study of Ageing (ELSA) final report*, London: Social Exclusion Unit, ODPM.

[40] Scharf, T. (2003) *Older people in deprived neighbourhoods: Social exclusion and quality of life in old age*, Swindon: ESRC Growing Older programme.

[41] Ibid.

[42] Third report from the Social Exclusion Unit, on deprived housing estates, 15 September 1998.

[43] Power, A., Hills, J., Sefton, T. and Stewart, K. (eds) (2009) 'New labour and unequal neighbourhoods', in *Towards a more equal society? Poverty, inequality and social policy since 1997*, Bristol: The Policy Press, pp 115–34.

[44] Holmes, C. (2006) *A new vision for housing*, London: Routledge.

[45] Barlow, J., Bartlett, K., Hooper, A. and Whitehead, C. (2002) *Land for housing: Current practice and future options*, the first of a series of papers from a Joseph Rowntree Foundation inquiry into Britain's housing in 2022, 19 March 2002.

[46] NHBC (National House-Building Council), *The Guardian*, 15 May 2009.

[47] Age Concern (2004) *Looking beyond the grey*, London: Age Concern.

TWO

Too tight to mention: unequal income in older age

Thomas Scharf

- Two-thirds of the working population are taxpayers; only two in five pensioners have enough income to pay tax.
- In 2006–7 the average income of the richest fifth of single pensioners was 279 per cent that of the poorest fifth.
- Forty-five per cent of people aged over 60 in deprived urban neighbourhoods were in poverty in one study, with over 67 per cent of Pakistani and 77 per cent of Somali older people in poverty.[1]

Poverty next to riches

The UK is one of the world's most affluent nations. According to the International Monetary Fund (IMF), the UK had a gross domestic product (GDP) per head of about US$36,500 in 2008, placing it above most other European countries, including France, Germany, Spain and Italy. Notwithstanding the economic downturn that began in 2008, the evidence shows that, over time, average incomes in the UK have increased substantially and the nation's wealth has continued to grow.

Against this background, it might seem puzzling to focus in this chapter so single-mindedly on issues relating to poverty and material disadvantage, but I do so for a straightforward reason. While it is clearly true that many older people have also benefited over time from the UK's increasing income and wealth, there is still a substantial minority whose lives are seriously diminished by the experience of financial hardship.

Over time, the gap between those older people who are better off and those who live in poverty has continued to widen.[2] The hard-won progress in reducing pensioner poverty has shown recent signs of stalling.[3] Moreover, poverty rates among older people are considerably higher in the UK than in many comparable European nations. In a nation as wealthy as the UK, such issues should be a matter of concern for all.

Lopsided policy

In this respect, it is perplexing that poverty in later life has not been accorded the same status as child poverty in recent years. One of the major achievements of the Labour government, elected to office in 1997, has undoubtedly been its concerted attempt to reduce poverty among children. Even though this policy is likely to fall short of its goal of eradicating child poverty by 2020, there has been a significant reduction in the numbers and proportions of children living in low-income households over the past decade.[4] There are obvious social justice arguments involved in tackling child poverty. On the one hand, it is seen as morally wrong in an affluent society like the UK that children should be disadvantaged by the low incomes of their parents. On the other, there is a broad consensus that steps should be taken to ensure that children have a fair start in life and the opportunity to make the most of their crucial formative years.

While forcefully expressed by organisations such as Help the Aged, Age Concern and the National Pensioners' Convention, equivalent arguments for tackling older people's poverty have not had the same political impact. It is difficult to understand why this is the case. It may reflect an institutionalised form of age discrimination, which places the needs of children and young people against those of older age groups. Or it might simply be that the age lobby, and those conducting research on this topic, have failed to get the argument across that equally valid social justice considerations apply in relation to older people and their financial circumstances.

For this reason, I will focus my attention in this chapter on presenting the research evidence relating to unequal incomes and their various impacts in later life as clearly as possible. I do this within the context of an overtly value-based approach to scientific enquiry, described in the next section. Moreover, drawing on a range of empirical studies undertaken with colleagues in recent years, I am devoting a substantial part of the chapter to illustrating just what it means to be living in poverty in old age in contemporary Britain. This is necessary, because debates about poverty and inequality have a tendency to lapse into the abstract, and often technical, discussion of general patterns and positions on income distribution. Experience suggests that giving a voice to those most affected by poverty is a crucial step in winning the argument for change. Having presented the evidence, I will then explore potential state responses to older people's poverty. The chapter concludes with a call for more concerted action to tackle poverty and to reduce income inequalities in later life.

Critical gerontology

It is still not that common for established social scientists to be quite so forthright when writing about issues to which they have devoted a considerable part of their academic lives. In this respect, a book such as *Unequal ageing* represents an open invitation to researchers to climb down from the fence and to declare where they stand on the issues at hand. I have little difficulty in doing this. It is a step that has long been advocated by gerontological researchers committed to a 'critical approach'. Proponents of critical gerontology include Martha Holstein and Meredith Minkler,[5] who recently argued that:

> [R]esearch cannot occupy a value-free realm: it means acknowledging that we all view the world – and do our research – with a view from somewhere. The view from nowhere – above the fray – does not exist any more in gerontological research than it does, for example, in physics. (p 19)

In this sense, my focus on the injustices associated with poverty in later life, and the wider issues of social exclusion and inequality, reflects a personal set of values and a commitment to improving the quality of older people's daily lives. I cannot claim that these ideas are especially original. Indeed, writing more than 20 years ago, Chris Phillipson and Alan Walker[6] eloquently spelled out 'the case for a critical gerontology'. In their view, critical gerontology represents 'a more value-committed approach to social gerontology – a commitment not just to understand the social construction of ageing but to change it' (p 12).

This critical perspective is especially relevant in relation to issues of unequal incomes and poverty in later life. It is capable of drawing attention to the ways in which disadvantage is structured by a range of social, economic and cultural processes. It provides opportunities for the voices of those affected by different forms of disadvantage to be heard in the public domain. It also highlights major issues of difference within older populations, characterised by such factors as age, gender, ethnicity, social class, health status and place of residence. In short, the critical perspective contrasts with one that – whether intentionally or not – homogenises the older population.

Diverse policy traditions

In international comparisons, especially those relating to its social and economic policies, the UK is often classified as a 'liberal' nation.[7] The liberal label tends to reflect a culturally based emphasis on the primacy of market-based solutions to emerging social problems reaching back to the origins of the British state. In countries such as the UK, the role of government has historically been to limit and regulate the potential excesses of the free market while simultaneously seeking to stimulate economic growth. This has been the broad approach of both Labour and Conservative administrations over the years.

Other nations have different, but equally entrenched, approaches to policy-making. For example, the Nordic nations tend to be grouped in what Castles[8] terms a social democratic 'family of nations'. In countries such as Sweden and Denmark state intervention has traditionally been accepted as a legitimate way of resolving social problems. Since the end of the Second World War these nations have actively sought to achieve equality between different social groups, using the welfare state as a means of promoting the idea of social citizenship. Countries such as Germany and France belong to a large cluster of European nations in which responsibility for meeting society's social obligations is shared by citizens, employing organisations and the state.[9]

Such traditions are important because they are reflected in the values that underpin public policy-making and the ways in which policies are subsequently shaped.

General wealth

In the case of the UK, the long-standing emphasis on the primacy of the free market has generated substantial inequalities in relation to the distribution of income and wealth. The degree to which the patterns of inequality have remained stable over time is remarkable. For example, there has been very little change in the overall distribution of wealth over the past three decades (see Table 2.1). The wealthiest tenth of the population still owns about half of all marketable wealth in the UK; the poorest half still owns less than one-tenth of the wealth. Those who are lower down the wealth distribution scale increasingly have a large share of their assets tied up in the home in which they live. When such housing wealth is ignored, the poorest half of the population owned just one per cent of all wealth in 2003. This represents a decline from 12 per cent in the mid-1970s.

Table 2.1: Distribution of wealth, 1976–2003, UK

Percentage of marketable wealth owned by:

	1976	1986	1996	2003
Most wealthy 1%	21	18	20	21
Most wealthy 5%	38	36	40	40
Most wealthy 10%	50	50	52	53
Most wealthy 25%	71	73	74	72
Most wealthy 50%	92	90	93	93

Percentage of marketable wealth less value of dwellings owned by:

	1976	1986	1996	2003
Most wealthy 1%	29	25	26	34
Most wealthy 5%	47	46	49	58
Most wealthy 10%	57	58	63	71
Most wealthy 25%	73	75	81	85
Most wealthy 50%	88	89	94	99

Net capital (£) required in 2003 to qualify for most wealthy percentages of population

1%	5%	10%	25%	50%
688,228	270,164	176,211	76,098	35,807

Source: HM Revenue & Customs

General income

A similar pattern applies when looking at the overall distribution of income (see Table 2.2). In 1994–5, the poorest fifth of the population received 5.8 per cent of the total income (after housing costs). In 2006–7 this proportion was almost unchanged, at 5.5 per cent, and had barely fluctuated in the intervening years. Similarly, the fifth of the population with the highest incomes received 43.1 per cent of total income in 1994–5 and 44.9 per cent in 2006–7. Other measures of income inequality show a fluctuating, if generally upward, pattern since the end of the 1970s.[10]

Income and wealth in later life

These general patterns represent the context for examining the financial circumstances of older people. In a country that is marked by such pronounced inequalities, it is not surprising that this is also reflected in the distribution of older people's incomes and wealth.

Table 2.2: Income shares (after housing costs), all households, 1994/5–2006/7, UK

Quintile shares of total income (in %)

	1994/5	1996/7	1997/8	1998/9	1999/2000	2001/2	2002/3	2004/05	2005/6	2006/7
Bottom 20% of the income distribution	5.8	5.9	5.8	5.9	5.8	5.9	6.0	6.0	5.7	5.5
Second quintile	11.3	11.2	11.3	11.1	11.2	11.5	11.6	11.7	11.5	11.5
Middle quintile	16.6	16.6	16.4	16.1	16.3	16.2	16.4	16.3	16.2	16.2
Fourth quintile	23.2	23.0	22.8	22.6	22.5	22.1	22.2	22.1	22.2	22.0
Top 20% of the income distribution	43.1	43.2	43.7	44.4	44.1	44.3	43.9	43.9	44.4	44.9

Source: Department for Work and Pensions (DWP) (2008) *Households Below Average Income: An analysis of the income distribution 1994/5–2006/7*, London: DWP.

Taking incomes as an example, the evidence shows that the likelihood of being in the top fifth of the income distribution is relatively low for pensioner households; after housing costs, 18 per cent of pensioner couples and 10 per cent of single pensioners were in the top income quintile in 2006–7. While pensioner households were less likely to be in the bottom fifth of the income distribution than other household types in 2006–7, single-pensioner households, and those of women in particular, were clustered in the bottom two-fifths.[11]

As in the overall income and wealth distribution, these data have remained fairly stable over time. This highlights the structural, entrenched nature of income inequalities and suggests that those who are consistently at the bottom of the income distribution have a heightened risk of living in persistent poverty. In this respect, there is a crucial difference between the poverty experienced by children and young people and that of older people: children born into poverty have a range of potential opportunities to escape their financial hardship – through education, training, employment, household formation or inheritance. Older people who enter retirement on a low income have very few opportunities to improve their financial circumstances. This is why the state has to assume a crucial role in relation to alleviating the poverty experienced by older people.

Questions about poverty and deprivation represent long-standing themes in research on ageing. Concern about the numbers of older people living in poverty found expression in the introduction of public pension systems in many European nations from the end of the 19th century. However, the subsequent development of modern welfare states did not always succeed in alleviating pensioner poverty. This was especially the case in the UK.

Despite the introduction of the basic state pension following the 1946 National Insurance Act, it was not too long before researchers such as Cole and Utting[12] and Townsend and Wedderburn[13] identified older people as being one of the largest groups still to be living in poverty. Poverty was seen disproportionately to affect widowed older people and those who lived alone. Most of these people were women, and many were aged 75 or over. Such entrenched patterns of material hardship provided a basis for the emergence of a critique of the very structures of inequality in later life.

'Structured dependency'

In particular, political economy perspectives on ageing from the late 1970s[14] sought to link poverty in old age to the social construction of lifelong inequalities based on class, generation, gender and ethnicity.[15] In this context, Peter Townsend[16] argued that growing old is affected by a form of 'structured dependency', produced by the imposition of retirement, poverty and restricted social roles. These ideas continue to be influential in UK research on ageing, notwithstanding a recent shift of focus towards the seeming relative affluence of newly retiring birth cohorts.[17]

Comparable research has remained fairly uncommon in other European nations, largely because the problem of older people's poverty appeared to have been resolved in the post-war period through public pension reform. However, the focus on poverty in later life has remained a central feature of UK gerontology.[18] The interest of the scientific communities in such issues corresponds closely with the growing risk of poverty experienced by older people from the mid-1980s.

Relative poverty

The proportion of pensioners experiencing relative poverty, defined as earning less than 60 per cent of contemporary household income, rose steadily through the period of Conservative government in the 1980s and 1990s. According to the analysis of pensioner incomes undertaken by the Institute for Fiscal Studies:[19]

> Over the second half of the 1980s ... relative pensioner
> poverty – measured by the proportion of pensioners on
> incomes below 60 per cent median [after housing costs]
> income – more than tripled, from around 13 per cent in
> 1984 to about 41 per cent in 1989. The rate then fell back
> sharply again over the early 1990s to about 26 per cent in
> 1993–4.

Progress under Labour

The general trend in the years following Labour's election to office in
1997 has been downward, whatever the measure of poverty used (see
Table 2.3). Although the proportion of pensioners living in poverty
peaked at 29 per cent in 1998–9, since then it has fallen back to 17
per cent in 2005–6, taking the comparative measure of income that
excludes housing costs. There is scope for debate about which measure
of income poverty is most appropriate: whether 'before housing costs',
which typically shows more modest progress with pensioner poverty,
or 'after housing costs', used more often by government, which could
be said to reflect disposable income more fully.

Table 2.3: Poverty rates for older people, 1996/7–2007/8, UK

Percentage of pensioners falling below various thresholds of contemporary
median income

	Before housing costs Below median			After housing costs Below median		
	50%	60%	70%	50%	60%	70%
1996/7	13	25	40	13	29	39
1997/8	13	25	40	13	29	38
1998/99	14	27	41	13	29	38
1999/2000	14	25	40	13	28	38
2000/1	13	25	39	11	26	36
2001/2	14	25	39	11	26	37
2002/3	13	24	39	11	24	37
2003/4	12	23	36	10	21	34
2004/5	11	21	34	8	18	30
2005/6	11	21	33	8	17	29
2006/7	13	23	35	10	19	31
2007/8	13	23	34	10	18	29

Source: DWP (2009) *Households Below Average Income: An analysis of the income distribution
1994/5–2007/8*, London: DWP.

However, the welcome progress may have stalled. According to recent data, both before and after housing costs pensioner poverty actually rose two percentage points, to 23 and 19 per cent respectively in 2006–7.[20] The introduction of Pension Credit in 2003, building on support added by the Minimum Income Guarantee, together with age-related payments in 2004, had continued the steady downward pressure on poverty under the Labour government. This was particularly commendable during the earlier period of the administration when increasing general prosperity, paradoxically, made it harder to reduce poverty. The withdrawal of age-related payments in 2006–7 appears now to have had a significant adverse impact on the trend of a decade.

The demographic impact

It is important to analyse poverty in terms of proportions of the population because that perhaps gives a fairer recognition of effort and impact than the absolute numbers. This is especially true when the population is ageing and the numbers of older people in poverty are likely to grow with that demographic trend. Having said that, it is salutary to remind ourselves that we are tolerating a situation where over two million older people (and two-and-a-half million on the before-housing costs measure) are living on a level of income which prevents them from taking a full part in life around them, at a time in life when they are more likely to need extra financial help to maintain a healthy diet, adequate warmth and comfort, and the semblance of a social life.

Poverty in Europe

The UK situation does not compare favourably with that of other European nations (see Table 2.4). In his analysis of a range of European data sources, Zaidi[21] established that the UK was one of a number of nations in which over a quarter of people aged 65 and over were living in poverty. Only Cyprus, Ireland, Spain, Portugal and Greece had higher proportions of this age group at risk of poverty at the time of this particular analysis. In all EU countries, poverty is more commonly experienced by women and also increases with age.[22]

Such data further emphasise the structured nature of poverty in later life. Old age and poverty do not have to go hand-in-hand, as is disproportionately the case in the UK. Other countries appear to be doing much better in minimising the risk of older people's poverty, often reflecting a concern to promote equality within society as a whole and between the generations in particular.

Table 2.4: Poverty rates for people aged 65 and above, 2003, EU countries

Country	At-risk-of-poverty rate* (%)	Population at risk of poverty (000s)
Cyprus	52	44
Ireland	40	176
Spain	30	2,112
Portugal	29	504
Greece	28	539
United Kingdom	24	2,268
Belgium	21	370
Malta	20	9
Slovenia	19	56
Austria	17	213
Denmark	17	135
Estonia	17	37
Finland	17	135
France	16	1,561
Italy	16	1,743
Germany	15	2,167
Latvia	14	52
Sweden	14	215
Lithuania	12	61
Slovakia	11	68
Hungary	10	156
Netherlands	7	154
Luxembourg	6	4
Poland	6	294
Czech Republic	4	57
EU25	**18**	**13,350**

* Poverty measure based on 60% of equivalised median household income.

Source: Zaidi, A. (2006) *Poverty of elderly people in EU25*, Vienna: European Centre

Poverty in later life: a life less equal

Over time, colleagues and I at Keele have been involved in a range of studies that have explored older people's experiences of poverty and disadvantage.[23] Alongside the necessary statistical data, such as that presented above, we have sought to capture the views of people who live in financial hardship. This reflects a commitment to bringing to the fore the voices of individual men and women whose personal stories can illuminate policy and academic debates. The people we have talked to over the years are often forthright in their views about the conditions in which they are living. Many have told us that their later years are rather different from the retirement that they had looked forward to during their adult lives. It is also evident from our studies that financial insecurity prevents people from leading the sort of lives that most people in an affluent society such as the UK would take for granted.

What poverty really means

To illustrate this point, I would like to draw on some findings from a study undertaken in disadvantaged communities in three major English cities.[24] Alongside a survey, the study involved detailed, in-depth interviews with a large number of people aged 60 and over. In this study we were able to show that very high proportions of older people living in such communities were living in poverty. However, that is only part of the picture. When looking at differences between those living in poverty and those whose material resources were more favourable, we can identify the contrasting lives of these two groups (see Table 2.5). Poverty in later life means cutting back on the basics of life, including food, fuel and the telephone. For some it means borrowing money from family and friends and, in isolated cases, looking for support from pawnbrokers and moneylenders.

Table 2.5: The two worlds of financial security: comparisons of older people in and out of poverty

	Older people not in poverty (n=321)	Older people in poverty (n=261)	All (n=582)
Is without a credit card	65%	88%	75%
Has gone without items because of shortage of money	15%	72%	41%
Has used the telephone less	6%	38%	20%
Has used less gas	4%	35%	18%
Has used less electricity	3%	35%	17%
Has been seriously behind with bills	3%	33%	17%
Has lived in poverty often or for most of life	9%	27%	17%
Is finding it (very) difficult to manage financially	4%	23%	13%
Has borrowed money from family	4%	18%	10%
Has borrowed money from friends	1%	16%	8%
Has borrowed money from moneylender	1%	4%	2%
Has borrowed money from pawnbroker	>1%	2%	1%

Case study: 'Flora Peters'

The in-depth interviews arising from this study offer particularly powerful evidence of the ways in which the experience of poverty affects daily life. Even when presenting this type of data there is a tendency to lose sight of the individual experience. For this reason, I would like to focus on the experience of one woman's life. While clearly an individual case, our other data suggest that this case is by no means unusual. The interview with someone we have called Flora Peters in our reports[25] was a follow-up interview with a person who had already taken part in the survey phase of our work.

At the time of interview, Mrs Peters was aged 61 and living in a small bungalow in Liverpool. Of mixed British and Indian origin, she looked much older than her 61 years. A widow with five children living locally, she reported a very difficult life history and had poor relationships with family members, including her children. Until the age of 35, Mrs Peters had worked as a machinist in a factory. However, she opted to leave work to raise her children. The premature death of her husband, coupled with her own deteriorating health, had prevented her from returning to work. As a consequence, Mrs Peters had entered retirement with very limited financial resources. Her health was poor, and she reported spending many days indoors, asleep on the couch in her front room.

Living on a low income affected many aspects of Mrs Peters' life, including her ability to pay for food, household bills and the upkeep of her home. In the survey phase of the study she had told us she could not afford to buy fresh fruit and vegetables, an outfit for special occasions, to replace broken electrical items, or to put money aside for a rainy day. Nor could she afford to have a holiday, to join in celebrations on special occasions such as birthdays, or to invite friends or family round for a meal or snack. She had been behind in her rent, indicated that she had lived in poverty for most of her life, and was currently finding it very difficult to manage on her income. These are all key indicators of poverty and reflect society's views about the types of resources that people should have access to.[26]

A structured survey can only tell so much about a person's life, generating an often unidimensional view of the research participant. The in-depth interview allows the researcher to put together a much fuller picture, and bring the participant to life. Visiting someone in their home also gives the researcher an opportunity to describe a participant's circumstances in the field notes:

> 'The interview was conducted in the living room. This room was in need of some decoration and was furnished cheaply. The carpets were thin and threadbare. The paintwork and electric sockets were dirty. There were isolated photos on the walls, but it wasn't possible to discern the identities of those portrayed. The room was warmed by an old-style electric fire with mock logs. Draped over the "logs" to air was a pair of tights. The atmosphere was very smoky and there were two bright pink plastic, freestanding ashtrays strategically located by the settee and Mrs Peters' armchair.'

The impact of poverty on Mrs Peters' daily life resonated throughout our conversation. In relation to food, for example, she described how she would sometimes go for days at a time without eating properly. She attributed this not only to a lack of financial resources, but also to a growing lack of interest in eating:

> FP: '[When shopping] I go in for the cheap stuff…. I can't afford the expensive stuff.'

TS: 'What sort of expensive stuff would you like to have?'

FP: 'I'd like to have a lot of things. I just couldn't afford them. I mean I can't afford steak and I used to love that. I go for the cheap bread because I just can't afford the dear bread.... The only time I have a really decent meal is a Sunday. I love my Sunday dinner.'

Mrs Peters also spoke about sometimes not bothering to eat at all. On occasion she would cook her Sunday dinner and then tip it into the bin, saying: 'As long as I have a smoke and a cup of tea I'm all right.' But things clearly were not all right. After having told me how she bought all her clothes from second-hand shops, and how she had spent the £10 a friend had given her on a pair of shoes, she said: 'Sometimes it makes you wonder whether it's worth living.'

Lack of income affected Mrs Peters' ability to enjoy a social life:

FP: '[I] can't afford to go to bingo.'

TS: 'Is that something you'd like to do?'

FP: 'I'd love to go to the bingo but I just can't afford it. I mean, I only get £78 a week now and then I've got gas and electric, there's nothing left.'

TS: 'Do you find it quite difficult to manage?'

FP: 'Yeah.'

Mrs Peters described managing to pay most of her bills, but was selective about which she chose to pay and never paid her water bill. But doing something about low income is not always easy for people who live in poverty – the benefits system appears complex and sometimes inaccessible:

TS: 'Have you ever tried to get any extra help?'

FP: 'No.'

TS: 'You wouldn't do that?'

FP: 'No.'

TS: 'You know, 'cause some people sort of would go and try and get Income Support or Housing Benefit.'

FP: 'I get Income Support, I get Housing Benefit, but I've still got to pay £13 a week on top of my rent because they said I was in arrears. I don't know how I'm in arrears because the Social pay my rent.'

Given her financial circumstances, the poor condition of her health and a difficult set of personal relationships, it should come as no surprise to hear that Mrs Peters reported having a very poor quality of life. The constant daily struggle occasionally appeared to be too much to cope with: 'I've sat here, cried my eyes out and I thought, well, I've got tablets there, I'll take them.'

Poverty is chronic

I have used Mrs Peters' powerful account because this clearly delineates the structural processes that have contributed to her disadvantage, and are reflected in her poor physical and mental health, and ultimately a diminished quality of life. Mrs Peters had lived in poverty for almost all of her life, and was entering old age without any form of financial security. In this sense, her poverty could be viewed as a chronic condition. In the gerontological literature, there is a growing focus on the idea of cumulative disadvantage, which is a useful concept in highlighting the ways in which disadvantages are accumulated over the life course and transported into old age.[27] Equally, the transition into old age itself can generate disadvantage, not least owing to the inadequacies of the basic state pension and of the means-tested benefits that prop it up. Some of these processes are captured in Mrs Peters' story.

Poverty is pervasive

Mrs Peters' example also indicates that poverty is not just about income. Indeed, much of our research over the past few years has tried to show how poverty is just one element of a wider set of interlocking disadvantages that many older people have to contend with.[28] Alan and Carol Walker[29] refer to social exclusion as being 'the dynamic process of being shut out, fully or partially, from any of the social, economic, political and cultural systems which determine the social integration of a person in society' (p 8). In developing a better understanding of the multidimensional nature of social exclusion, we have shown how poverty frequently interacts with other forms of disadvantage to reduce older people's life chances and to diminish in significant ways the quality of their lives.[30]

Older poverty is unequal

As noted earlier, across the UK there are countless people living in similar circumstances to Mrs Peters. Official data suggest that there are more than two million pensioners living in households with incomes that are below 60 per cent of average income. Two-thirds of these low-income pensioners are women; women living alone and those aged 75 and over are at particular risk of poverty.[31] Poverty disproportionately affects older people belonging to minority ethnic groups – with the Department for Work and Pensions reporting poverty rates of 43 per cent for older Pakistani and Bangladeshi people and 28 per cent for Black Caribbean older people.[32] In one of our studies, almost eight out of ten older Somali people and seven out of ten older Pakistani people were living in poverty.[33] Poverty rates vary across the UK, and are highest in Northern Ireland.

Combating inequality

Measures of relative poverty tell one specific story of limited resources in later life. Measures such as the Gini coefficient tell the important story of inequality in income. Figure 2.1 below plots the trend of inequality for the retired and non-retired population over the last 30 years. The evidence shows that inequality is consistently lower for the retired population than for those still in work. This arises simply because

Figure 2.1: The Gini coefficient of income inequality, retired and non-retired households, 1977–2005/6, UK

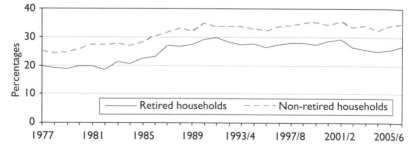

Note: The Gini coefficient is a measure of statistical dispersion most prominently used as a measure of inequality of income distribution or inequality of wealth distribution. It is defined as a ratio with values between 0 and 1: a low Gini coefficient indicates more equal income or wealth distribution, while a high Gini coefficient indicates more unequal distribution.

a narrower range of income possibilities exist when people are by and large no longer earning a salary.

What stands out clearly from this analysis, though, is the success achieved by the government between 2001 and 2005 in reducing inequality and poverty for older people. The more marked and consistent trend in comparison with the working population can largely be attributed to positive improvements in state benefits, such as one-off enhancements to the basic state pension and the introduction of Pension Credit. Such success should be instructive for future efforts to reduce both poverty and inequality.

Inequality in Europe

We lack the same ability to critique older age inequality across Europe. However, given the mirroring of general inequality that we have observed in the above analysis, it might be reasonable to assume that the UK's performance in relation to older age inequality follows the same pattern as shown below in Figure 2.2.

The recession

Meanwhile, the effects of the severe global and domestic recession threaten to undo much of the material improvement in the position of older people. Older people are particularly vulnerable to fluctuations in energy prices, which force unhealthy choices upon them. The vivid complaint expressed in the dilemma 'heating or eating?' may now be familiar, but it has not yet galvanised effective action to remedy the problem of poverty and associated ill health, such as that leading to what are euphemistically referred to as 'excess winter deaths' – the more than 20,000 older people who die each winter in the UK as a result of low temperatures.[34]

While many older people have no savings to speak of, those who have any are badly affected by low interest rates, which have caused the levels of annuities available to plummet.

Policy responses

Independent studies[35] have acknowledged the efforts made by the Labour government to reshape the UK's pensions architecture and in so doing to reduce pensioner poverty. This has primarily been achieved through a stronger focus on means-tested benefits. As noted, the generally downward trend in 'after housing costs' relative poverty

Figure 2.2: Gini coefficients of income inequality, 2006, EU countries

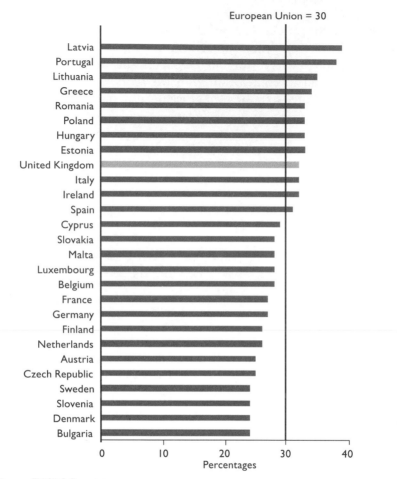

Source: EU-SILC, Eurostat

is striking and commendable. There has also been a decline in recent years in persistent poverty – arguably a compelling indicator of impact, reflecting as it does the grinding-down effect of living on a limited income. State pension reforms to increase access to the full basic state pension, to link its uprating to earnings and to encourage pension saving in employment are all likely to make a valuable difference in the years ahead.

Nevertheless, despite such positive measures, projections by the Institute for Fiscal Studies[36] (see Figure 2.3) suggest that, even allowing for the effect of planned state pension reforms, pensioner poverty will not fall significantly between now and 2017.

Figure 2.3: 'Actual' and simulated poverty rates among those aged 65+ (under White Paper reforms) for 50%, 60% and 70% median poverty thresholds, 1996/7–2017/18, UK

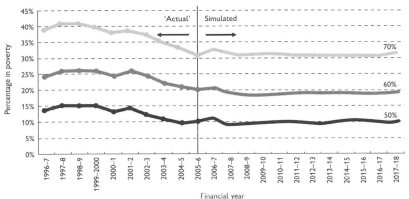

Notes: Simulations are based on 'White Paper policies'. The 60% poverty threshold has been calibrated in 2005–6 so that the proportion of the simulated sample of individuals in ELSA aged 65+ in England in poverty is equal to the proportion of a comparable sample drawn from the official *Households Below Average Income* dataset who have incomes below 60% of the population median. The 50% and 70% thresholds have been calculated by scaling this 60% poverty threshold. All thresholds are then increased by 1.8% in real terms in successive years.

And as far as inequality is concerned, the widespread trend away from Defined Benefit pension schemes and towards Defined Contribution schemes, with the associated individualisation of risk and outcomes, is likely to result in even greater inequality of pension income over time.

Routes out of poverty

One potential route out of poverty in later life is through the various state benefits that top up individuals' pension entitlements. Recent research suggests that, if claimed, these benefits would in fact enable older people to reach a level of decency in income.[37] Through a detailed study of people's perceived needs in relation to normal household expenses on essentials, it was established that pensioners who actually claim and receive their Pension Credit entitlements manage to attain an acceptable standard of living.

The problem of under-claiming

However, estimates suggest that between 33 and 41 per cent of people of state pension age fail to claim their entitlement to Pension Credit.[38] A result of the under-claiming of this and other benefits is that as much as £5.1 billion of means-tested (that is, excluding disability) benefits may well be going unclaimed each year in the UK. While recent government policy has made considerable progress in simplifying the procedure of claiming benefits, many older people are simply unable or unwilling to undergo the means-testing that underpins the receipt of Housing and Council Tax Benefits and the pension credits designed to top up the basic state pension.[39] One reason for failing to claim benefits was reported by Townsend[40] in his classic study *The family life of old people*. Speaking about her unwillingness to claim additional state benefits, one of his female respondents made the following comment:

> 'I've never liked to cadge. I'm not one to go running for help. I don't spend money. I manage on what I've got. I don't smoke, don't drink, and I've never been used to eating much. I've never been used to it. I'm not a cadger. I've never been that way brought up.' (p 183)

Such views continue to be held by many older people. Generally, official research classifies 'perceived ineligibility' as the primary explanation for non-claiming. People simply do not connect with the sense that they are entitled to claim benefits. Moreover, some older people are bound to distrust the well-intentioned efforts of the Pension, Disability and Carers' Service that exhort them to claim, given a growing suspicion about random communications offering potentially handsome prizes out of the blue. (An average under-claim of £28 a week may not be handsome, but it can make a big difference to someone living on a low fixed income.)

Even more strenuous efforts seem then to be needed to reach those who fail to claim their entitlement. Some moves have been made in this direction. The 2008 Welfare Reform Act facilitated the piloting of automatic payment of benefits. Automatic payment depends for its accuracy on sharing between the relevant agencies personal data about levels of income. This is a delicate subject, in the aftermath of cases of computers and discs from government departments going missing. However, it is the nettle to be grasped if targeting the poorest is to work better as a policy. The experience of benefits advice work in recent years also suggests that face-to-face advice, and the involvement of local community groups, are more effective in reaching the most disadvantaged communities.

Poor – or just getting by?

However, we should not become fixated by artificial dividing lines between 'the poor' and 'the rest'. Even if they claimed all of the benefits to which they are entitled, a considerable number of older people would still be struggling to cope at the margins of poverty. This is because so many of them have incomes that are just above the poverty threshold: 1.3 million pensioners are within 10 per cent of the official poverty line.[41]

Year in, year out

Moreover, once older people become poor, there is relatively little that they can do about this without significant intervention by the state. Ninety per cent of pensioners living below the poverty line are living in persistent poverty: that means that they have lived in a household with a low income in at least three years out of a four-year period.[42] These proportions barely changed for much of the 1990s, pointing to the existence of a core group of older people – people like Mrs Peters – for whom poverty is a chronic problem (see Table 2.6).

Table 2.6: Persistent poverty of older people, 1994–2005, UK

Percentage of pensioners falling below various thresholds of contemporary median income in at least 3 out of 4 years

	Before housing costs Below median		After housing costs Below median	
	60%	70%	60%	70%
1994–7	19	35	19	34
1995–8	19	35	21	33
1996–9	20	36	21	33
1997–2000	20	37	22	34
1998–2001	21	37	22	34
1999–2002	19	37	18	33
2000–3	18	34	16	31
2001–4	16	34	15	30
2002–5	15	31	13	27

Source: DWP (2008) *Households Below Average Income: An analysis of the income distribution 1994/5–2006/7*, London: DWP.

Challenging poverty in later life: the need for reform

Having presented the research evidence, I would like in the final section to sketch out some potential strategies for dealing with poverty in later life. Here, I return to my opening comments, since this is where the value-orientated, critical gerontology perspective diverges from more traditional approaches. In calling for a 'passionate scholarship', Holstein and Minkler[43] express the following sentiment:'We hold out this hope for those of us committed to critical gerontology ... that we do whatever we do with passion and a belief that our scholarship can make a difference: that is move people to action' (p 26). The need for action in relation to many older people's low incomes in the UK is evident. There is clearly a lot to be done, but in some ways the task ahead might seem relatively straightforward.

Building on success

Policy-makers and politicians would struggle to claim that they do not know how to address the issues associated with income inequalities and poverty in later life. In fact, a major step forward would be for government to put into place some of the good intentions identified in a range of policy documents over recent years. The Department for Work and Pensions' (2005) *Opportunity Age: Meeting the challenges of ageing in the 21st century*[44] and the Social Exclusion Unit's (2006) *A sure start to later life: Ending inequalities for older people*[45] reports represented a significant step in the right direction and gave initial cause for optimism. However, the political will to translate the aspirations of these policies into action has, in my view, been far too limited.

A sure start to later life, for example, was one of the final acts of the now disbanded Social Exclusion Unit. As yet, those at the heart of government seeking to champion age are not breaking through and managing to promote sufficiently co-ordinated thinking in ageing policy. The Public Service Agreement relating to older people (PSA 17) specifically refers to tackling pensioner poverty 'through paying pensions and benefits to those eligible, so that pensioners continue to share in the rising prosperity of the nation'. However, the focus on ensuring that people receive their pension and benefit entitlements fails to address the structural reasons that underpin the poverty experienced by many older people.

The heart of the matter: reforming the basic state pension

However much we look to recent policy reforms or pilot schemes, the evidence that I have presented – and that is borne out in countless other studies – points to the structural causes that underpin poverty in old age. This requires a more fundamental change in policy – one which shifts attention away from a narrow focus on improving benefits take-up and piecemeal efforts at increasing pensioners' income by measures such as Pension Credit or the Winter Fuel Allowance, towards a significant change in the universal basic state pension.

Older people often have low incomes because they have lived in poverty during their adult lives, and perhaps also during their childhood. While there is clearly a need for government action at earlier stages of the life course, the only way in which many of the two million older men and women who are living in poverty in the UK can escape this experience is by government intervention. Uprating the basic state pension – which even in its full entitlement amounts to only 16 per cent of average earnings   to at least the Guarantee Credit level of Pension Credit would represent a major shift away from means-testing and would ensure that many older people were automatically lifted out of financial hardship.

A question of justice

This type of approach is something that the age lobby has advocated for many years now. But the argument has always foundered, amid a welter of official reports, on the basis of cost. After all, how can a nation whose older population is growing so quickly afford to meet the perceived growing pension burden? In my view, cost is only part of the issue, and probably not the main part at that. After all, Britain spends proportionally rather less on its basic state pension than most other advanced industrial nations, and this is not predicted to change much over the decades ahead.

The real issues are structural and relate to the unequal distribution of income and wealth in Britain described in earlier sections of this chapter. Against the background of a highly unequal society, the fundamental question remains one of social justice. How, as a society, can we tolerate a situation in which so many older people's daily lives are blighted by the challenge of trying to make ends meet? A society in which government press releases suggest that the 25,300 excess winter deaths of 2007/8 is a figure which 'remains low'?[46] It may not currently be politically fashionable, but an obvious solution would be a renewed focus on the redistribution of society's resources.

Ironically, the economic downturn that began with the financial crisis of 2008 may represent an excellent opportunity for the state to intervene more directly to reduce income inequalities in later life. The failure of the unregulated free market to deliver security in later life, including security for many people who have saved for their retirement through occupational and personal pensions linked to stock markets, cries out for the necessary security to be guaranteed by the state.

The overarching objective of the ageing lobby, and also of researchers committed to the critical gerontology approach, has to be to secure a national commitment to ending older people's poverty, and to tackling the structural sources of inequality. This objective can only be met by a reorientation in social policy towards a recognition of the value of a universally provided basic state pension. In my view, the joint challenge of the ageing lobby and critical gerontology is, therefore, to win the political rather than the economic argument.

Five things we can do now

1. Ten years after the child poverty declaration, make a government commitment to end pensioner poverty by 2030, supported by public take-up targets.
2. Set 2015 as the target date for raising the basic state pension to the level of the Guarantee Credit.
3. Boost work programmes with local community groups and face-to-face advice services to ensure that older people belonging to black and minority ethnic groups, and other groups most acutely affected by poverty, receive their full state pension and benefit entitlements.
4. Improve co-ordination of policy-making and services for older people by rolling out the LinkAge Plus pilot projects to all of England.
5. Take further steps to simplify the process of claiming benefit entitlements, and within two years mainstream the pilots on automatic payment of benefits set up under the 2008 Welfare Reform Bill.

Notes

[1] Scharf, T., Phillipson, C., Smith, A.E. and Kingston, P. (2002) *Growing older in socially deprived areas: Social exclusion in later life*, London: Help the Aged.

[2] Darton, D. and Strelitz, J. (2003) *Tackling UK poverty and disadvantage in the 21st century*, York: Joseph Rowntree Foundation.

[3] DWP (Department for Work and Pensions) (2008) *Households Below Average Income – 1994/5 to 2006/7*, London: DWP, Information Analysis Directorate.

[4] Palmer, G., MacInnes, T. and Kenway, P. (2008) *Monitoring poverty and social exclusion 2008*, York: New Policy Institute and Joseph Rowntree Foundation.

[5] Holstein, M. and Minkler, M. (2007) 'Critical gerontology: reflections for the 21st century', in M. Bernard and T. Scharf (eds) *Critical perspectives on ageing societies*, Bristol: The Policy Press, pp 13–26.

[6] Phillipson, C. and Walker, A. (1987) 'The case for a critical gerontology', in S. DeGregorio (ed) *Social gerontology: New directions*, London: Croom Helm, pp 1–15.

[7] For example, Esping-Andersen, G. (1990) *The three worlds of welfare capitalism*, Cambridge: Polity Press; Castles, F.G. (1993) *Families of nations: Patterns of public policy in Western democracies*, Dartmouth: Aldershot.

[8] Castles, F.G. (1993) *Families of nations: Patterns of public policy in Western democracies*, Dartmouth: Aldershot.

[9] Hill, M. (2006) *Social policy in the modern world: A comparative text*, Oxford: Blackwell.

[10] Hills, J. (1998) *Income and wealth: The latest evidence*, York: Joseph Rowntree Foundation; Wilkinson, R. and Pickett, K. (2009) *The spirit level: Why more equal societies almost always do better*, London: Allen Lane.

[11] DWP (Department for Work and Pensions) (2008) *Households Below Average Income – 1994/5 to 2006/7*, London: DWP, Information Analysis Directorate.

[12] Cole, D. and Utting, W. (1962) *The economic circumstances of old people*, Welwyn: Codicote Press.

[13] Townsend, P. and Wedderburn, D. (1965) *The aged in the welfare state*, London: Bell.

[14] Walker, A. (1980) 'The social creation of poverty and dependence in old age', *Journal of Social Policy*, vol 9, pp 49–75; Phillipson, C. (1982) *Capitalism and the construction of old age*, London: Macmillan.

[15] Minkler, M. and Estes, C. (eds) (1999) *Critical gerontology*, New York: Baywood Press.

[16] Townsend, P. (1981) 'The structured dependency of the elderly: the creation of policy in the twentieth century', *Ageing and Society*, vol 1, no 1, pp 5–28.

[17] Gilleard, C. and Higgs, P. (2005) *Contexts of ageing: Class, culture and cohort*, Cambridge: Polity Press.

[18] For example, Scharf, T., Phillipson, C., Smith, A.E. and Kingston, P. (2002) *Growing older in socially deprived areas: Social exclusion in later life*, London: Help the Aged; Burholt, V. and Windle, G. (2006) *The material resources and well-being of older people*, York: Joseph Rowntree Foundation; Price, D. (2006) 'The poverty

of older people in the UK', *Journal of Social Work Practice*, vol 20, no 3, pp 251–66; Scharf, T., Bartlam, B., Hislop, J., Bernard, M., Dunning, A. and Sim, J. (2006) *Necessities of life: Older people's experiences of poverty*, London: Help the Aged; Naegele, G. and Walker, A. (2007) 'Social protection: incomes, poverty and the reform of pension systems', in J. Bond, S. Peace, F. Dittmann-Kohli and G. Westerhof (eds) *Ageing in society*, 3rd edn, London: Sage Publications.

[19] Goodman, A., Myck, M. and Shephard, A. (2003) *Sharing the nation's prosperity? Pensioner poverty in Britain*, IFS Commentary 93, London: Institute for Fiscal Studies.

[20] DWP (Department for Work and Pensions) (2008) *Households Below Average Income – 1994/5 to 2006/7*, London: DWP, Information Analysis Directorate.

[21] Zaidi, A. (2006) *Poverty of elderly people in EU25*, Vienna: European Centre.

[22] Naegele, G. and Walker, A. (2007) 'Social protection: incomes, poverty and the reform of pension systems', in J. Bond, S. Peace, F. Dittmann-Kohli and G. Westerhof (eds) *Ageing in society*, 3rd edn, London: Sage Publications; European Commission (2008) *Monitoring progress towards the objectives of the European Strategy for Social Protection and Social Inclusion*, Brussels: European Commission.

[23] Scharf, T., Phillipson, C., Smith, A.E. and Kingston, P. (2002) *Growing older in socially deprived areas: Social exclusion in later life*, London: Help the Aged; Scharf, T. and Bartlam, B. (2006) *Rural disadvantage: Quality of life and disadvantage amongst older people – A pilot study*, London: Commission for Rural Communities; Scharf, T., Bartlam, B., Hislop, J., Bernard, M., Dunning, A. and Sim, J. (2006) *Necessities of life: Older people's experiences of poverty*, London: Help the Aged.

[24] Scharf, T., Phillipson, C., Smith, A.E. and Kingston, P. (2002) *Growing older in socially deprived areas: Social exclusion in later life*, London: Help the Aged.

[25] See also Scharf, T., Phillipson, C. and Smith, A.E. (2005) *Multiple exclusion and quality of life amongst excluded older people in disadvantaged neighbourhoods*, London: Social Exclusion Unit, Office of the Deputy Prime Minister.

[26] Gordon, D. et al (2000) *Poverty and social exclusion in Britain*, York: Joseph Rowntree Foundation; Pantazis, C., Gordon, D. and Levitas, R. (eds) (2006) *Poverty and social exclusion in Britain: The Millennium Survey*, Bristol: The Policy Press; Scharf, T., Bartlam, B., Hislop, J., Bernard, M., Dunning, A. and Sim, J. (2006) *Necessities of life: Older people's experiences of poverty*, London: Help the Aged.

[27] Crystal, S. and Shea, D. (1990) 'Cumulative advantage, cumulative disadvantage, and inequality among elderly people', *The Gerontologist*, vol 30, no 4, pp 437–43; Dannefer, D. (2003) 'Cumulative advantage/disadvantage and the life course: cross-fertilizing age and social science theory', *Journals of Gerontology B*, vol 58, no 6, pp S327–37.

[28] Scharf, T., Phillipson, C., Smith, A.E. and Kingston, P. (2002) *Growing older in socially deprived areas: Social exclusion in later life*, London: Help the Aged.

[29] Walker, A. and Walker, C. (eds) (1997) *Britain divided: The growth of social exclusion in the 1980s and 1990s*, London: Child Poverty Action Group.

[30] For example, Scharf, T., Phillipson, C. and Smith, A.E. (2005) *Multiple exclusion and quality of life amongst excluded older people in disadvantaged neighbourhoods*, London: Social Exclusion Unit, Office of the Deputy Prime Minister.

[31] DWP (Department for Work and Pensions) (2008) *Households Below Average Income — 1994/5 to 2006/7*, London: DWP, Information Analysis Directorate.

[32] Ibid.

[33] Scharf, T., Phillipson, C., Smith, A.E. and Kingston, P. (2002) *Growing older in socially deprived areas: Social exclusion in later life*, London: Help the Aged.

[34] Brock, A. (2008) 'Excess winter mortality in England and Wales, 2007/8 (provisional) and 2006/7 (final)', *Health Statistics Quarterly*, vol 40, pp 66–71.

[35] Evandrou, M. and Falkingham, J. (2009) 'Pensions and income security in later life', in J. Hills, T. Sefton and K. Stewart (eds) *Towards a more equal society? Poverty, inequality and policy since 1997*, Bristol: The Policy Press.

[36] Brewer, M., Browne, J., Emmerson, C., Goodman, A., Muriel, A. and Tetlow, G. (2007) *Pensioner poverty over the next decade: What role for tax and benefit reform?*, IFS Commentary 103, London: Institute for Fiscal Studies.

[37] Bradshaw, J., Middleton, S., Davis, A. et al (2008) *A minimum income standard for Britain: What people think*, York: Joseph Rowntree Foundation.

[38] DWP (Department for Work and Pensions) (2008) *Income-related benefits: Estimates of take-up in 2006–7*, London: DWP Analytical Services Division.

[39] Phillipson, C. and Scharf, T. (2004) *The impact of government policy on social exclusion of older people: A review of the literature*, London: Social Exclusion Unit, Office of the Deputy Prime Minister.

[40] Townsend, P. (1957) *The family life of old people*, Harmondsworth: Penguin.

[41] Help the Aged (2007) *Pensioner poverty: Help the Aged policy statement 2007*, London: Help the Aged.

[42] Scharf, T., Bartlam, B., Hislop, J., Bernard, M., Dunning, A. and Sim, J. (2006) *Necessities of life: Older people's experiences of poverty*, London: Help the Aged.

[43] Holstein, M. and Minkler, M. (2007) 'Critical gerontology: reflections for the 21st century', in M. Bernard and T. Scharf (eds) *Critical perspectives on ageing societies*, Bristol: The Policy Press, pp 13–26.

[44] DWP (Department for Work and Pensions) (2005) *Opportunity Age: Meeting the challenges of ageing in the 21st century*, London: DWP.

[45] Social Exclusion Unit (2006) *A sure start to later life: Ending inequalities for older people*, London: Social Exclusion Unit, Office of the Deputy Prime Minister.

[46] ONS (Office for National Statistics) (2008) 'Excess winter deaths remain low in 2007/8', News release, 27 November.

THREE

The uneven dividend: health and well-being in later life

Anna Coote

- Almost 98 per cent of people with dementia in the UK are over 65; its prevalence doubles with every five-year increase across the age range, but only one-third of those with dementia receive a formal diagnosis.
- The poorest older people are:
  - over five times more likely than the richest to have poor general health
  - about five times more likely to have difficulty walking
  - twice as likely to have diabetes
  - more than twice as likely as people under 50 to die.

The asset of health

Health is a precious resource. It is a basic need, shared by all human beings in every country of the world.[1] Our state of health strongly influences our ability to enjoy life, to participate in society and to fulfil our potential, as well as the way we feel about ourselves and – often – how others feel about us.

In later life, more than at any other time except perhaps in the few months after we are born, health is a critical factor that defines us, enables us and constrains us. It determines what growing old means to us. How old we feel and act can depend to a large extent on our mental and physical health.

Defining health

What is health, exactly? It has been defined as 'a state of complete physical, mental and social well-being, and not merely the absence of disease or infirmity', and as a 'fundamental human right'.[2]

The state of our health is measured most often in terms of how long we live and whether we suffer from one or more mental or physical illnesses. Physical, mental and social well-being are closely related and can be mutually reinforcing. So, for example, if we have a positive attitude to life and feel good about ourselves, we are more likely to have enjoyable relationships with other people that are health-enhancing, and less likely to suffer from physical disease. Conversely, being physically unwell can isolate us from others and make us feel anxious and depressed, possibly triggering further illness.

Unequal health

Although everyone needs health, not everyone enjoys it in the same measure. Indeed, there are gross inequalities in the way health is distributed across the human population, both between countries and within countries, and between different groups and neighbourhoods.

This chapter is about inequalities in health. It focuses mainly on inequalities between different social groups because these are the most marked and persistent and preventable. It considers how these inequalities affect people's experience as they grow older and how growing older can compound health inequalities. It examines the causes of health inequalities and considers what can be done to narrow health inequalities.

Living longer ...

People live longer, healthier lives in Britain today than they did half a century ago, and the general trend continues towards improvement. But health inequalities between social groups and between people living in different parts of the country have been increasing. If we compare the life expectancy of those in the highest and lowest social classes, we find that, in the 1970s, women in the top group lived 4.8 years longer than women at the bottom of the scale, while men in the top group lived 5.4 years longer than men at the bottom. Twenty years on, the figures were, respectively, 6.3 and 9.4 years. So the gap widened in the last two decades of the 20th century by nearly two years for women and by four years for men.[3]

And the pattern is global. The Commission on Social Determinants of Health, set up by the World Health Organization (WHO), reported in 2008 that 'within countries, the differences in life chances are dramatic and are seen worldwide. The poorest of the poor have high levels of illness and premature mortality.'[4]

The New Labour government arrived in 1997 with a strong commitment to reduce health inequalities, but its efforts have shown few positive results. Inequalities in life expectancy for women rose steeply between 2002 and 2005, mainly because of dramatic improvements for women in the top social class. For men during that time, health inequalities measured by social class have been gradually levelling out, with the fastest rates of improvement for unskilled manual workers.[5]

... in better health?

As time goes by each generation gets a chance of living longer than the last one. In just two decades between 1981 and 2002, life expectancy for those aged 65 and over increased by three years for men and two years for women. If you made it through to the age of 65 by 2002, you could expect to live to be 84 if you were female and 81 if you were male.[6] The trouble is that health is not improving at the same rate as life expectancy. At 65 a man can expect to live another 16.9 years and a woman 19.7 years, but in each case that is expected to include, on average, more than four years of ill health. And the poorer we are, the more likely we are to be ill in those extra years.

With each passing year, perhaps inevitably, our assessment of our own health gets a little less sanguine. That is a universal trend. But the timing and speed of this deterioration varies with social and economic circumstances. Poor people's health starts to decline earlier and then gets worse more rapidly. A study of men aged 45–65 found that the level of incapacity experienced by men in the lowest social class by their mid-50s was not reached by men in the top class until their mid-60s. In other words, the process known as 'functional ageing' tends to begin about 10 years earlier in poorer groups, with men and women in disadvantaged circumstances ageing more quickly than their better-off contemporaries.[7]

There are signs that these patterns are intensifying. There has been a steady increase in self-reported poor health for all social groups, but the sharpest rise has been for women in the lowest group, between 2000 and 2005. Objective measures confirm that inequalities have persisted and increased. Over the last decade inequalities among women have worsened dramatically across a range of conditions, including obesity, mental ill health and cardiovascular disease.[8]

The ills of age

- **Impaired vision:** in the UK 42 per cent of over-75s will develop cataracts, and almost 50 per cent will have age-related macular degeneration
- **Hearing loss:** at 50 the proportion of deaf people increases sharply: 55 per cent of over-60s have a hearing impairment
- **Physical strength:** 17 per cent of men and 27 per cent of women aged 65–69 scored as 'impaired' when tested, rising to 73 per cent and 85 per cent of those aged over 85
- **Mobility and access:** 10 per cent of over-75s have difficulty getting to the local supermarket and 17 per cent to the local hospital; nearly half of those aged over 70 have difficulty getting out and about
- **Osteoporosis:** one in two women and one in five men over 50 will break a bone, at least partly because of osteoporosis
- **Osteoarthritis:** 10–20 per cent of those over 65 are affected – eight million people across the UK
- **Stroke:** in England, every year, more than 100,000 strokes occur; 75 per cent of these affect people aged over 65
- **Incontinence:** bladder problems rise with age to 16 per cent of men and 19 per cent of women aged 65–69, and a third of those over 85 reporting such problems
- **Depression:** about one-sixth of people over 65, and an estimated 40 per cent of those in care homes, have depression at any one time
- **Dementia:** nearly 98 per cent of people with dementia in the UK are aged over 65

Fair care

In a key recommendation for tackling health inequalities, WHO calls for 'universal healthcare', based on 'principles of equity, prevention and health promotion' and ensuring 'access regardless of ability to pay'.[9] This is a more crucial matter for countries that lack basic healthcare than for the UK, which has enjoyed a universal health service since 1948. But is the National Health Service (NHS) equitable as well as universal? After all, health services must not only help to prevent illness, but also – crucially – provide treatment where prevention fails.

Where the NHS is concerned, there is some evidence that people who are poor and old do not enjoy the same access to or quality of service as those who are younger and better off. This has been explained by difficulties in attracting good clinical staff to disadvantaged neighbourhoods, by the attitudes and expectations of clinicians and patients, and by uncertain science and questionable economics.[10]

Research by the National Consumer Council found in 2004 that an over-emphasis in government policy on reducing NHS waiting lists had worsened the health equality gap between rich and poor, and that the universal character of the service was being undermined: 'It is no longer true to say that people's access to a comprehensive range of healthcare is based on clinical need, rather than how much they can afford.'[11]

Dignity in care

A recent study of 18 countries including the UK found that older people were subject to inequitable treatment in health services and attributed this to three main factors: 'many physicians' documented ageism; 'uncertainty and ambiguity about appropriateness and effectiveness of medical treatments in older patients ... [and] debatable and not entirely scientifically based cost-effectiveness ceilings set by economists' studies for the prevention of human suffering and death that deny older people needed medical treatments'.[12]

A survey for Help the Aged in 2008 showed that 64 per cent of adults think older people are not always treated with dignity by health and social care professionals;[13] 44 per cent think these professionals do not involve older people in decisions about their treatment[14] and 29 per cent of older adults think that health professionals consider older patients a nuisance.[15] It seems that poverty and age combine to compound inequalities in healthcare as well as in health. And although the government has stressed the vital importance of 'dignity', recruiting thousands of 'dignity champions' across the health service, this key aspect of how older people are cared for remains more of a slogan than a measured and managed imperative in service delivery.

Health inequalities matter

Why do health inequalities matter? First and most obviously, people who are already disadvantaged in social and economic terms bear a heavier risk of ill health than those who are better off. And those risks tend to accumulate over the life cycle. Illness can exacerbate social and economic disadvantage – for example, by preventing us from getting out and about, or looking after ourselves, or earning a living or a decent pension. It can undermine our capacity to be resourceful when the going gets tough, and blight our later years. In short, older people are more likely to suffer a triple burden of poverty, isolation and illness.

Second, health inequalities affect the whole of society, not just the poor. The Commission on Social Determinants of Health was at pains to emphasise that the problem is not confined to those worst off. 'In countries at all levels of income, health and illness follow a social gradient: the lower the socio-economic position, the worse the health.'[16] Furthermore, unequal societies are less successful than more equal ones, with more ill health, more crime, lower levels of trust and higher levels of stress – all of which damage the lives of people at every level, including the rich.[17]

Third, health inequalities carry heavy costs for the healthcare system and hence for the taxpayer. If everyone enjoyed the same average good health as people in the highest socio-economic group, the costs of running the NHS could be cut significantly. So health inequalities are unethical, unjust, dysfunctional and wasteful. Given the huge costs of the NHS (close to £100 billion a year, according to the Department of Health's *Departmental report 2008*), the fierce downward pressure on public spending in times of recession, and the hefty carbon footprint of the NHS, health inequalities are unsustainable.

They are also preventable – because most ill health can be prevented and because the factors that make poorer people more vulnerable to ill health are also preventable.

Preventing health inequalities

Action to prevent illness can be taken at different levels. Good clinical treatment, such as a daily aspirin to thin the blood, or cataract removal, or a hip replacement, can stop a minor health problem becoming a disabling or life-threatening one. Screening – for breast cancer, for example – can prompt early diagnosis so that illness can be treated before it gets serious (but not if, as at present, the automatic recall for screening stops in a person's early 70s, just as the risk accelerates). Vaccination and immunisation programmes help to prevent the spread of disease.

Advice and information can be given to people about what to do to safeguard and improve their health: this is about changing behaviour – encouraging individuals to eat nutritious food, take exercise, practise safe sex and avoid harmful substances such as tobacco, too much alcohol and illegal drugs. It can also be about telling people how to seek help if they already have a problem that threatens their health, such as domestic violence, an addiction or an eating disorder.

Health systems and governmental organisations tend to focus on clinical prevention and on efforts to change behaviour. At the time of writing, more than three million people were taking statins, the cholesterol-lowering drugs that help prevent heart disease. There are proposals to extend the prescription to 6–7 million people, costing the NHS some £250 million a year.[18] Meanwhile, health information advertisements that are currently circulating warn of the dangers of sexually transmitted diseases, and tell us how to spot early signs of a stroke. We are all familiar with the government's efforts to stop people smoking and drinking too much alcohol.

These forms of prevention are important and effective, up to a point. Statins, for example, can cut the risks of a heart-related death by 45 per cent. Anti-smoking campaigns have cut the proportion of smokers since 1970 from 55 to 22 per cent for men and from 44 to 20 per cent for women.[19] However, they only go so far.

Clinical treatments happen 'downstream' when risks to health have already arisen. They may be the only or the best way to prevent a problem from getting worse, depending on the circumstances, but medicine takes control of the condition, with its inevitable costs and sometimes undesirable side-effects, including some negative impacts of pharmaceuticals on physical and mental health, and patients' own loss of power over what happens to their minds and bodies. The underlying causes of illness remain undisturbed.

Underlying causes of deteriorating health

When it comes to changing behaviour, advice and information from official sources affect different social groups in different ways. WHO has identified three major risk factors that make people vulnerable to chronic diseases such as heart disease, stroke, cancer, chronic respiratory diseases and diabetes. These are: unhealthy diet, physical inactivity and tobacco use. If these risks were eliminated, says WHO, at least eight in ten cases of heart disease, stroke and type-2 diabetes would be prevented, as well as four in ten cases of cancer.[20]

Health awareness: reinforcing health inequalities?

But although diet, exercise and tobacco use may seem to be a matter of lifestyle 'choices', people who are better off almost invariably eat more nutritious food, take more exercise and are more likely to refrain from smoking. For example, before the dangers of cigarette smoking were widely known, smoking prevalence varied little by socio-economic group. Today there are clear differences, not least because social groups respond differently to health information campaigns. By 2005, 29 per cent of adults in manual occupations smoked compared to 19 per cent in non-manual occupations. According to Cancer Research UK, smoking is a key contributory factor to health inequalities between socio-economic groups in the UK, and accounts for a major part of the differences in life expectancy between manual and non-manual groups.[21]

This is not because the poor are careless about their health, but because social and economic conditions powerfully influence the options we all have at our disposal. It is easier for well-off people to make healthy choices. This brings us to the next – and most important – level at which ill health can be prevented: changing the underlying factors that influence behaviour.

Poverty, health and choice

Sometimes the conditions that shape our options are predominantly practical – for example, when there is no money to buy fresh vegetables, or no shop in the neighbourhood that sells them. Often our preferences have more complicated roots, built up over time by customs and habits that are formed by social, economic and cultural experience. A young mother 'chooses' to smoke because her mother always has, or because it gives a sense of rhythm to her days, which are otherwise relentless, or because it feels like the only thing she can do just for herself. A retired couple 'choose' to take the bus instead of walking half a mile to the shops because they are fearful of being out on the streets, or they have seldom felt a pleasure in walking and no one else they know would walk half a mile at their age. An elderly man 'chooses' to eat chips and biscuits most days because they are foods he enjoys and feels he can trust.

WHO confirms that, in all countries, the poor are more vulnerable to chronic disease not only because of unhealthy behaviour but also because of 'material deprivation, psychosocial stress ... unhealthy living conditions and limited access to good-quality health care'. These other factors undermine our health directly, and also edit the 'choices' we make about things that affect our health, such as diet, physical activity and tobacco use.[22]

Causes and life courses

It is more complicated still. Our chances of living longer and healthier lives are influenced by factors well beyond our control. Hilary Graham, who has traced the development of health inequalities through the life cycle, concludes that 'people's current health is related to their current circumstances in the early years, through childhood, and across early adulthood and older age'.[23] Children, she observes, are uniquely sensitive, both before and after birth, to environmental influences, which are shaped by family background. Those born into disadvantage start life with a 'poorer platform of health', which may compromise their physical growth and cognitive development, impairing their confidence and progress at school, with major consequences for their adult lives. Combined social and health inequalities over the life cycle 'increase the risk of both poverty and early onset of impairment and illness':

> By middle age, class inequalities appear to be already deeply etched into the ageing process. Both early life disadvantage and current disadvantage are linked to an earlier and more rapid decline in health. As sociologists have noted, 'the body is the most ubiquitous signifier of class'.[24]

Mental health and well-being

The impact of poverty and disadvantage over the life cycle is similar for mental illness. Children in the poorest households are three times more likely to have mental health problems than children in well-off households; unemployed people are twice as likely to suffer from depression as people in work.[25] More than two million people over the age of 65 in England have symptoms of depression,[26] which can be triggered by poor health, money worries, losing a loved one and stressful events such as moving into a care home.[27] Yet the response to the mental health threats in later life ranges from the inadequate to the downright ageist: from poor diagnosis of dementia to fatalistic inertia in offering help with depression.

People with mental illness are often stigmatised and socially isolated, which exacerbates the problem. Not only does mental illness affect poor people more often, but it also increases vulnerability to physical illness. Depression, for example, has been found to endanger health more than four major chronic conditions: angina, arthritis, asthma and diabetes.[28]

Poor diet and lack of physical exercise are recognised risk factors for mental as well as for physical health, and people who suffer from depression and anxiety often find it harder to give up smoking. So the same cycle of social and economic disadvantage, unhealthy choices and vulnerability to illness can be seen here too.

What can be done to reduce health inequalities?

Health inequalities are preventable because poverty and the conditions that usually go with it are preventable. WHO's Commission on Social Determinants of Health makes three overarching recommendations to achieve health equity within a generation.

The first is to 'improve daily living conditions', which includes putting 'major emphasis on early child development' and 'creating conditions for a flourishing older life'. The second is to 'tackle the inequitable distribution of power, money and resources' such as inequities between women and men, which requires strengthened governance for 'people across society to agree public interests and reinvest in the value of collective action'. The third is to 'measure and understand the problem and assess the impact of action' which includes a 'stronger focus on social determinants in public health research'.[29]

These proposals are global. What can be done in the UK? I suggest there are three areas where major changes are needed. First, there must be changes to social and economic conditions to enable everyone to have a fair and equitable chance of living a long and healthy life. Second, there must be fundamental changes to the health system, so that it gives priority to preventing illness and promoting health, and builds up its capacity to give high-quality care to people with unavoidable illnesses, regardless of their age or circumstances. Third, there must be changes in opportunities and expectations associated with growing older, so that people have a better chance of enjoying good health in their later years.

Changing social and economic conditions

Poverty is arguably the most significant cause of inequalities in health and well-being. It is well beyond the scope of this chapter to examine options for ending poverty in the UK, but here are some key pointers.

Tackling poverty and income inequality

The links between poverty and illness affect us right across the life cycle, and even across generations. The health of parents before they conceive a child can influence that child's life chances; the mother's health in pregnancy is vitally important. In order to narrow health inequalities for older people, poverty must be tackled for all age groups.

Everyone should have enough to live on. This is complicated. What is 'enough'? In Chapter Two Thomas Scharf explored the issue of decency in income levels. The challenge of both determining and then delivering adequate material wealth is profound and underpins every dimension of unequal ageing.

Most people in paid employment are entitled to the National Minimum Wage, now £5.73 an hour for over-22s, which has been enshrined in law since 1998, reviewed annually by the Low Pay Commission. This makes it possible to earn just over £200 for a 35-hour week: far from generous, but a step in the right direction. The basic state pension, for someone who has paid all the necessary contributions, is £95.25 a week and Jobseeker's Allowance for over-25s is £64.30 a week.[30]

For most other state benefits and tax credits, there is a maze of wide-ranging rules, variations and compliance criteria. These flow from different and sometimes conflicting norms and imperatives: to identify and assist the 'deserving' poor; to eliminate child poverty; to support carers; to root out 'scrounging'; and to get the jobless into paid work. Partly as a result of these complexities, far too many people fail to claim or receive their legal entitlements – because they do not know how to operate the system, or cannot comprehend the rules and regulations, or want to avoid the stigma of claiming. A nation that is capable of estimating and enforcing payment of a fair living wage is manifestly incapable of estimating or ensuring payment and receipt of a fair living income. Finding that capability may be the surest way of narrowing health inequalities for all, including older people.

On a global scale, poverty is both an absolute and a relative factor. People at the bottom of the socio-economic scale in rich countries may be considered enviably well-off by others living in much poorer countries, yet at the same time suffer acutely from the experience of relative poverty at home. Their lives may not be directly threatened by lack of essential food, water and healthcare, but their physical and mental well-being may be seriously impaired – because they have so much less than others, because they are usually relatively powerless and are often led to doubt their own worth. This applies across the social gradient, with health improving in line with rising socio economic status. What matters, then, is not just making sure that everyone has enough, nor even just narrowing the gap between rich and poor (as if that were not enough of a challenge), but levelling the gradient between social groups.

As things stand today, a part-time medical practitioner can earn more than six times the minimum wage, with median pay at £38.78 an hour. A middle-earning company director can earn 20 times the basic pension, with median pay at £1,878 a week.[31] In the league of income inequalities the UK ranks higher than every other 'developed' country except Singapore, the US and Portugal.[32] As I have noted, health and social problems are much more strongly linked with income inequalities than with average national income per person.[33] So the aim must be to constrain high levels of income and wealth, as well as to raise the income of the poorest. It is high time to review rates of tax for those with higher earned and unearned incomes.

Redistributing time and carbon

Looking forward, there may be other, no less effective, ways of redistributing the means of living well. When the global economy is in deep recession and dole queues are lengthening daily, the case for a shorter working week, with fewer paid jobs spread among more people, demands attention. Shorter hours can make it easier for people to combine paid employment and caring responsibilities, reducing stress, anxiety and family problems that make people more vulnerable to illness, especially in poorer families. Security at work, as well as more flexible and family-friendly working conditions across the life course, will help to reduce risks to health. But in order to tackle health inequalities, it will be crucial for these to be equally available to low-paid and part-time workers.

As the prospect of catastrophic environmental damage looms larger with every new scientific forecast,[34] the case for enforced carbon reduction becomes increasingly urgent. No one has yet developed an entirely plausible model for reducing individual carbon emissions in line with ambitious new government targets. But a model will need to be found in the very near future and it could help to narrow inequalities – for example, by reducing non-essential consumption which is largely associated with affluence, by a carbon trading system that favours the poor, or by some combination of similar measures. But if carbon reduction is approached by raising energy prices or taxing carbon, these are likely to penalise the poor and widen inequalities.

Social justice and the 'social wage'

Since the mid-1940s, the means of living well have been redistributed through the welfare state, including education, health and social care, and other public services, which are available free or partly subsidised and funded through taxation. These have been called the 'social wage'.

Arguably, the second most effective way of tackling health inequalities (after fighting poverty and narrowing income inequalities) is to ensure that these services are excellent for all social groups. Education and childcare are especially important because, if standards are high enough, they can counteract some effects of income inequality and help to build opportunities for children from poor backgrounds to lead long and healthy lives.

As we describe through this book, the quality of housing and the character of neighbourhoods are also vital. Insecure tenure, overcrowding, damp, poor insulation, noise, graffiti, litter, broken windows, fear of crime, lack of control, poor management and policing, lack of trees, busy roads, poor access to shops, parks and play spaces, isolation and disconnectedness – these are all bad for health.

Secure, congenial, well-insulated and ventilated homes, clean, safe neighbourhoods, participative governance, good local management, effective local policing, shared open spaces and amenities, well-tended, accessible parks and play areas, local shops selling good, fresh food, streets with little or no motorised traffic that encourage walking and cycling – these are all good for health.

How we experience public services and daily life at neighbourhood level will affect our health throughout our lives and, as we have seen, the effects accumulate over the life cycle. High-quality services, homes and neighbourhoods can help to reduce relative poverty and to compensate for earlier disadvantage. But what happens too often is that poor people get poorer services and find themselves powerless to escape from living conditions that perpetuate poverty and disadvantage.

How can this have happened after 60 years of peace and plenty in a democratic welfare state? Part of the answer to this highly complex problem can be found in three related political ideas that have strongly influenced planning and delivery of public services, particularly since 1979: individualism, choice and targeting.

In a nutshell these purvey the notion that individuals who are vulnerable and needy are themselves the 'problem' to be fixed. Where publicly funded services are concerned, the politically sanctioned approach to improving standards and enabling individuals to get what they need has been to encourage them to choose from a range of competing options. And the preferred way to deal with poverty and cycles of deprivation has been to target successive government interventions on poor and disadvantaged neighbourhoods.

Together, these ideas endorse market principles and mechanisms that compound inequalities, blame the poor for their predicament, sidestep the systemic roots of the problem and sideline the principle of collective responsibility for a shared destiny. What is at stake here is not just how to improve the quality of services, but how to shift the ideological underpinnings so that the 'social wage' can do more to promote social justice.

Legislation on equalities

At the time of writing, a new Equality Bill was making its way through Parliament, designed to bring together all existing anti-discrimination legislation and strengthen some aspects of legal protection. It will seek to make age discrimination unlawful in the provision of goods, facilities and services. The Government Equalities Office insists 'this is not about stopping older people enjoying free bus passes, but about tackling unjustifiable age discrimination where it has negative consequences'. The Bill also creates a single equality duty that will 'require public bodies to consider the diverse needs and requirements of their workforce, and the communities they serve, when developing employment policies and when planning services'.

Legislation is no panacea for inequalities, but it can certainly help to provide official endorsement, to change the climate of opinion and encourage more equal treatment, as well as preventing more obvious expressions of unfair treatment.

In what may be a last radical gasp before a change of government in 2010, the Government Equalities Office has been 'taking steps to understand other forms of inequality, and the role they play in determining people's chances in life'. These include 'factors like family background, educational attainment, where you live, and the sort of job you have [which] can influence your chances in life as well as things like gender, ethnic background, and whether or not you have a disability'.

The minister responsible, the Rt Hon Harriet Harman QC MP, set up a National Equality Panel in 2008, chaired by Professor John Hills of the London School of Economics and Political Science, to analyse links between social class and the categories such as age, gender, race and disability that are traditionally covered by anti-discrimination law.[35]

In a parallel move, the Health Secretary Alan Johnson MP commissioned Professor Sir Michael Marmot, who had chaired the WHO Commission on Social Determinants of Health, 'to conduct an independent review to propose the most effective strategies for reducing health inequalities in England from 2010'.[36]

Both inquiries are due to report in 2009 and to inform subsequent policy-making. It is hard to predict what effect they will have, but together they should cast a useful spotlight on the underlying causes of health inequalities and, possibly, help shift the policy paradigm away from individualism, choice and targeting.

Changing the health system

In gathering evidence for his review of health inequalities, Professor Marmot set up nine task groups to address different themes. These covered children's services, employment, social protection, the built environment, sustainable development, economics, public health interventions, delivery systems and social exclusion. It is telling that not one of these focused exclusively on the NHS. Only the groups on public health and delivery systems were concerned as part of their brief with what health services could do to reduce health inequalities. The widely used 'rainbow model of health' (see Figure 3.1) confirms the limited but significant role played by health services.[37]

Figure 3.1: The rainbow model of health

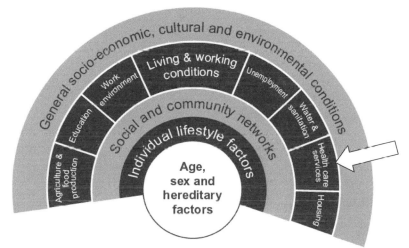

Source: Dahlgren, G. and Whitehead, M. (1991) *Policies and strategies to promote social equity in health*, Stockholm: Institute for Futures Studies

There are nevertheless important ways in which the health system could improve its performance in tackling health inequalities. As with other public services, the driving force behind health service policy over the last decade has been an ideological commitment to individualism (or 'personalisation'), choice and targeting. Giving patients a 'choice' of general practitioner and where to go for hospital care has been accorded higher priority than promoting better health for all.

Broadly speaking, people want 'choice' when services they receive without choice are not good enough. And, as noted above, poorer people tend to get poorer services; at the same time, people's freedom to choose can be seriously impaired by the options that are available to them and by their capacity to negotiate official procedures. On both counts, the offer of choice tends to favour the better-off and will do little to help narrow inequalities.

Targets have been set for reducing health inequalities (measured by life expectancy and infant mortality), but for most of the last decade a higher priority has been given to targets for avoiding deaths by cancer and cardiovascular disease, reducing waiting times and (more recently) stopping the spread of hospital-acquired infections. These have focused on 'downstream' clinical interventions, rather than on the underlying causes of illness; the aim has been to achieve numerical scores regardless of the socio-economic background of the individuals concerned, and it is usually more difficult, for reasons discussed earlier, to 'save lives' where there are multiple risks including poverty, powerless and social disadvantage.

The NHS could improve its contribution to reducing health inequality by developing a much stronger focus on preventing illness among lower socio-economic groups, investing more in primary care services, dramatically improving access to preventative primary care services for people in disadvantaged areas and – crucially – sustaining such developments over time. These are already among the objectives of the Labour government, which has gone some way towards shifting resources into primary care and has paid much closer attention to addressing the causes of illness than previous administrations. There have been major campaigns to reduce smoking, notably by banning smoking in public places, and to tackle obesity. It will take time for any positive effects to reverse current trends towards widening inequalities. Much will depend on whether this level of commitment can be sustained through any future changes of government.

Only profound change will do

Much will also depend on whether the UK health system can achieve and sustain a profound shift in its culture, from one dominated by the power and ethos of the medical professions to one that aims to keep the whole of the population well and reduce levels of dependence on clinical intervention. I suggest three principled changes: a whole-systems approach to well-being for all, an equal partnership between citizens and health workers, and saving the best for the rest.

A service for well-being

It is worth recalling that health has been defined as 'a state of complete physical, mental and social well-being, and not merely the absence of disease or infirmity' and 'a fundamental human right'.[38] A commitment to this ideal has been regularly reaffirmed by international health organisations, but it is not strongly reflected in the way the UK health system conducts its affairs. Health and social care are organised separately. Mental and physical health are diagnosed and treated by separate cohorts of specialists. Healthcare organisations are primarily dedicated to treating illness. We rarely see a doctor unless we are already ill. The professionals with the highest status and pay, who wield the most power in the health system, are those who specialise in treating complex medical and surgical conditions, not those who work at community level to keep people well.

A system that focused on well-being for all would be very different. It would be concerned as a matter of urgency with enabling people to feel good about themselves and in control of their lives, to have a positive outlook and strong social connections, to be active and curious, and to have and fulfil a sense of purpose. Professionals would be trained to understand the whole person, not just this or that disembodied organ. In effect, the system would be turned on its head. Caring for people and looking after psychological and social well-being would have a far higher priority and status. So would measures aimed at preventing illness and safeguarding and improving physical health. Illness would be a sign that the system had failed, not merely a chance for highly paid clinicians to display their virtuosity.

With a focus on well-being for all, a central aim would be to enable every individual to have the best possible chance of being well, regardless of their background or circumstance. A whole-systems approach would address the underlying determinants of well-being across the life cycle, preventing the accumulation of risks to health that hastens the ageing process for those who are poor and disadvantaged. In other words, it would be a system designed for and geared towards reducing health inequalities.

Equal partnership

I have argued elsewhere[39] that public services cannot go on expanding with ever-growing tax revenues from continuing economic growth. If we want decent services in future we shall need to find other resources. The potential for growth lies in human resources that are embedded in the everyday lives of every individual (time, wisdom, experience, energy, knowledge, skills) and in the relationships between them (love, empathy, watchfulness, care, reciprocity, teaching and learning).

These assets and relationships, described as the 'core economy', are routinely overlooked and undervalued by policy-makers and practitioners.[40] Yet they are central and essential to society. They underpin the market economy, by raising children, caring for people who are ill, frail and disabled, feeding families, maintaining households and building and sustaining intimacies, friendships, social networks and civil society. They can flourish and expand, or weaken and decline, depending on the circumstances and conditions within which they operate. The core economy can 'grow' to provide fresh input to healthcare if these human resources are recognised, valued, nurtured and supported.

A key mechanism for growing the core economy is to introduce *co-production* into the design and delivery of public services.[41] This goes well beyond the idea of 'citizen engagement' or 'service user involvement' to foster the principle of equal partnership. It changes the dynamic between the public and public service workers, so that they are no longer either 'providers' and 'users' or 'them and us'. Instead, the model recognises that everyone has assets, not just problems, acknowledging that 'we' have as much to contribute as 'they' do. People pool different kinds of knowledge and skills, based on lived experience and professional learning, so that they work together to co-produce well-being.

This approach engages previously unrecognised and under-used resources in delivering services. There is a real transfer of power from providers to users. Responsibility is shared – both for deciding what needs to be done and for subsequent action. Except where individuals' mental capacity is severely impaired, co-production can apply right across the age range.

A useful example of co-production in action is the 'care banks' that have been piloted in several areas, including the London Borough of Camden.[42] Individuals who require social care form a group with others who have similar needs and with carers and care workers. Together, they identify what they need and how to provide help to each other, using time as a measure of exchange, with everyone's time afforded equal value. Care workers act as brokers and facilitators, not just as caregivers. This model acknowledges that everyone has something to offer, brings in new resources in the form of time exchanged and helps to generate and support social networks.

Uncommodified exchanges of time and other human resources are already common in low-income areas where people are used to finding ways of helping one another, often because public services let them down. Importing co-production into the public sector will require a radical transformation of the way professionals are trained, how they understand their role and how they conduct themselves in practice. It also requires a fundamental shift in people's expectations of public services. But because it brings services so much closer to the people who are supposed to benefit from them and because it resonates with working-class traditions of mutual aid, it promises better results for poorer groups.

When people feel valued, have more control over their lives and stronger connections with each other, they are less vulnerable to ill health, and more likely to be physically and psychologically well. When people participate actively in defining and meeting their needs, the results are likely to be better than if others just do things for them or to them. Co-producing services and well-being can help to address health inequalities, prevent needs arising, achieve better outcomes, reduce unnecessary demands for services and so safeguard their long-term viability.

Saving the best for the rest

Reducing unnecessary demands by keeping people well should conserve resources and make it possible to provide better treatment and care for those with ill health that has not or cannot be avoided. One reason why the NHS seems so impossibly strapped for cash is that it spends more than half its budget treating preventable disease.

Most of us fall ill in our later years. What we need then is the best possible service. We want to be treated with dignity and respect, to be comfortable and well cared for, to be with people we know and trust, to be free from pain, to recover if possible and, if not, to be helped to survive as long as we want and to have a good death. The last six months apparently absorb 30–50 per cent of the total healthcare costs of our lifetime.[43] Yet end-of-life care is uncomfortably divided between expensive high-tech intervention and palliative care that remains a Cinderella service of patchy quality.

People who are poor cannot buy in extra help to cushion the effect. When hard-pressed families are caring for an elderly relative the experience, however rewarding in some respects, can draw them further into poverty, add stress and anxiety and increase their own risks of ill health. A significant shift of resources to improve the quality of treatment and care of older people and of palliative care – both by improving services and by giving more support to carers – should ensure that socio-economic status does not determine the quality of life in its final stages.

Rewriting the script: opportunities and expectations

Finally, and perhaps most importantly, much can and should be done to change the experience of growing older. The old adage 'you're as young as you feel' sums it up. How we feel depends on circumstance, opportunity, how we see ourselves and how others see us. How we feel will influence as well as be influenced by the state of our physical, psychological and social well-being.

I have noted that the process of 'functional ageing' starts 10 years earlier for those at the lower end of the socio-economic scale. What could narrow that gap? Reducing income disparities and improving childcare, education, employment opportunities and living conditions for those who are currently poor and powerless would address the social and economic determinants of health inequalities. High-quality preventative primary healthcare would provide useful support. In addition, opportunities for older people must be improved. Later and more flexible retirement, including the option of reduced hours and responsibilities, would help to change expectations and attitudes, provide more income, sustain health-enhancing mental and physical activity and continue important social relationships.

Breaking down the distinction between paid employment and volunteering would have a similar effect, enabling people already retired to get involved with others, do something useful and supplement their pensions. There should be more affordable channels for learning, for developing talents, refreshing expertise, acquiring new skills and passing on knowledge and skills to others.

Following the care bank example, there should be many more such opportunities to share experience, exchange favours and help one another. Walking, cycling, dancing and any kind of active physical exercise, preferably in green open spaces, should become a normal part of everyday life for all age groups in urban as well as rural areas. Housing policies should attach great importance to helping people live near friends and family members. But the key point is that, in every case, opportunities must be available to all social groups, especially to the poor.

We cannot hold back the advance of years, but we can acknowledge that ageing is, to a very large extent, a social construct. We have constructed a model of ageing that casts the over-60s as past-it pensioners, the over-70s as well over the hill, the over-80s as frail relics and the over-90s as stupendous survivors who really should shuffle off. And that is the diplomatic version. The poorer we are, and the poorer we have been throughout our lives, the more danger we are in of fitting these stereotypes. If we want to put an end to health inequalities for older people, we must change our perceptions of ageing and the way our services respond, as well as ensuring there are plentiful opportunities for staying active across the life course.

Five things we can do now

1. Create well-being services that break down the artificial boundaries between health, social care and community living, rooted in the principle of staying healthy and engaged.
2. Drive through a law for age equality in care, to empower older people, protect from ageism and use money better.
3. Re-energise the life course approach to maintaining health with 'health, wealth, well-being' reviews in mid-life, starting with the worst areas of inequality.
4. Put money behind services that involve communities and their resources of skills, energy and know-how.
5. Make detailed assessment of how far people feel they are treated with dignity a universal measure of compliance for care services.

Notes

[1] Doyal, L. and Gough, I. (1991) *A theory of human need*, Basingstoke: Palgrave.

[2] Declaration of Alma-Ata, International Conference on Primary Health Care, Alma-Ata, USSR, 6–12 September 1978.

[3] Sassi, F. (2009) 'Health inequalities: a persistent problem', in J. Hills, T. Sefton and K. Stewart (eds) *Towards a more equal society? Poverty, inequality and policy since 1997*, Bristol: The Policy Press, p 136.

[4] WHO (World Health Organization) Commission on Social Determinants of Health (2008), *Final Report: Executive summary*, Geneva: WHO.

[5] See note 3, Sassi (2009) op cit, pp 141–2.

[6] National Statistics: www.statistics.gov.uk/cci/nugget.asp?id=881.

[7] Graham, H. (2007) *Unequal lives: Health and socio-economic inequalities*, Milton Keynes: Open University Press, pp 156–7.

[8] See note 3, Sassi (2009) op cit, pp 148–55.

[9] WHO (World Health Organization) (2008) *Closing the gap in a generation: Health equity through actions on the social determinants of health*, Geneva: WHO, p 12.

[10] Wheeler, B., Shaw, M., Mitchell, R. and Dorling, D. (2005) *The relationship between poverty, affluence and area*, Findings, York: Joseph Rowntree Foundation, September.

[11] NCC (National Consumer Council) (2004) *Health services: Creeping charges in healthcare*, London: NCC.

[12] Safiliou, C. (2008) *Review of age inequalities in medical treatment*, Executive summary (www.50plus.gr/images/content/EXECUTIVE%20SUMMAR1-age-based%20inequalities%20in%20health%20care.doc).

[13] ICM Research Pain Survey for Help the Aged, unpublished, 2008.

[14] Ibid.

[15] Help the Aged (2008) *Spotlight report 2008: Spotlight on older people in the UK*, London: Help the Aged.

[16] Ibid.

[17] Wilkinson, R. and Pickett, K. (2009) *The spirit level: Why more equal societies almost always do better*, London: Allen Lane.

[18] Smith, R. (2009) 'Millions of statins will go to low-risk over-40s', *Daily Telegraph*, 10 February (www.telegraph.co.uk/health/healthnews/4573728/Millions-of-statins-will-go-to-low-risk-over-40s.html).

[19] Lung cancer and smoking statistics, Cancer Research UK (http://info.cancerresearchuk.org/cancerstats/types/lung/smoking/#percent).

[20] WHO (World Health Organization) (2005) *Preventing chronic diseases: A vital investment*, WHO global report (www.who.int/chp/chronic_disease_report/contents/en/index.html).

[21] See note 19, Cancer Research UK, op cit.

[22] WHO (World Health Organization) *Chronic diseases and health promotion* (www.who.int/chp/chronic_disease_report/part2_ch1/en/index14.html).

[23] See note 7, Graham, op cit, pp 158–9.

[24] Ibid, p 159.

[25] DH (Department of Health) (1999) *National Service Framework for mental health*, September, Standard One, p 14.

[26] Age Concern (2007) UK Inquiry into Mental Health and Well-Being in Later Life (www.ageconcern.org.uk/AgeConcern/F8888695C89A4E969E58D1C243F2A2B0.asp).

[27] Age Concern England (2008) *Out of sight, out of mind: Social exclusion behind closed doors*, London: Age Concern England, February.

[28] *The Lancet*, vol 370, 8 September 2007.

[29] WHO (World Health Organization) (2008) *Closing the gap in a generation: Health equity through actions on the social determinants of health*, Geneva: WHO.

[30] DWP (Department for Work and Pensions) 'Benefits uprating' (www.dwp. gov.uk/mediacentre/pressreleases/2008/dec/NewBenefitRates.pdf).

[31] National Statistics (2009) 'Patterns of pay', *Economic & Labour Market Review*, vol 3, no 3, March, p 29.

[32] See note 17, Wilkinson and Pickett, op cit, p 17.

[33] Ibid, pp 20–1.

[34] IPCC (Intergovernmental Panel on Climate Change), *Climate change 2007 synthesis report*, IPCC (www.ipcc.ch/pdf/assessment-report/ar4/syr/ar4 syr. pdf); Stern, N. (2009) *A blueprint for a safer planet: How to manage climate change and create a new era of progress and prosperity*, London: The Bodley Head.

[35] www.commonsleader.gov.uk/output/Page2657.asp

[36] Global Health Equity Group, UCL (2009) 'Strategic review of health inequalities in England post 2010 (Marmot Review)' (www.ucl.ac.uk/gheg/marmotreview).

[37] Dahlgren, G. and Whitehead, M. (1991) *Policies and strategies to promote social equity in health*, Stockholm: Institute for Futures Studies.

[38] Declaration of Alma-Ata, International Conference on Primary Health Care, Alma-Ata, USSR, 6–12 September 1978 (www.who.int/hpr/NPH/docs/declaration almaata.pdf).

[39] Coote, A. and Franklin, J. (2009) *Green well fair: Three economies for social justice*, London: New Economics Foundation.

[40] Ibid.

[41] For more detail see nef (New Economics Foundation) (2009) *A wealth of time*, London: nef; nef (2008) *A co-production manifesto*, London: nef.

[42] nef (New Economics Foundation) (2009) *A wealth of time*, London: nef.

[43] 'Cost of dying is biggest item in health care costs, actuaries tell Romanow', *Community Action*, 18 March 2002 (http://findarticles.com/p/articles/mi_m0LVZ/is_8_17/ai_84895824/?tag=content;col1).

FOUR

No place like home? Housing inequality in later life

Sue Adams

- Average male life expectancy at birth in the Lenzie district of Glasgow is 82; in the Calton district of the same city it is 54.[1]
- Of the two million homes in England in serious disrepair, 38 per cent are occupied by older people.[2]
- The number of disabled people in England is set to double by 2041; poorer older people are more likely to need adaptations to their homes to live independently.
- In remote rural areas 29 per cent of households in poverty contain someone over 60.

The importance of home

The quality of a home shapes quality of life. The physical condition of a person's home and the qualities of the neighbourhood in which they live influence their health and ability to be involved with their family, friends and social networks.[3] Housing suitability and standards play a key role in determining emotional well-being, including an individual's sense of engagement with, or exclusion from, wider society. Home is inextricably linked to personal identity, social status and sense of having control over one's life.[4] Quality and suitability of place are key determinants of the experience of growing older,[5] hence the centrality of housing and neighbourhood in the debate about age and inequality.

Throughout this book we explore how ageing can decline into a journey of loss, of different kinds, rather than one of gain and progressive fulfilment. This is certainly true in housing. Several studies highlight the fear of loss of control over where and how one lives in older age.[6]

The majority of older people say they want to remain in their own homes for as long as possible.[7] This has become a cornerstone of policies relating to older people's housing, health and social care. Enabling independent living and providing care at or closer to home are key objectives. So the quality and suitability of the homes of older people, and consequently the impact of inequality in housing, is key to this wider policy objective.

This chapter explores:

- the housing inequalities experienced by older people generally compared with other age groups
- the housing inequalities between different sectors of the older population
- emerging and necessary policy responses.

We are ageing ... and diverse

Today 30 per cent of households are headed by a person over retirement age and nearly half of all projected household growth up to 2026 will be older households.[8] The proportion of the population aged 60 years and over has increased dramatically, up from one in 25 in 1900 to one in five today. By 2020 this is predicted to reach one in four.[9] Increasing life expectancy is resulting in one of the most rapid rates of population growth in the numbers of the 'older old'. In 2004–5 the number of people over 85 reached 1.2 million. By 2025–6 this is predicted to almost double, to 2.3 million.[10]

The older population is also becoming increasingly diverse. For example, while the current age profile of black and minority ethnic (BME) communities is younger than that of the rest of the population,[11] this is set to change significantly over the next decade. This has particular implications for housing given the over-representation of BME groups in low-income, lower-equity, poorer-quality housing stock.[12]

Despite such significant demographic trends, the majority of regional housing strategies and regional spatial strategies (the major determinants of housing expenditure and wider planning priorities) barely mention older people, age inequality or age-related social trends.[13] Housing expenditure continues to be focused on new-build family housing or the so-called 'economically active' younger age groups, and all too often regeneration is youth-focused, with older people ignored or marginalised.[14]

Contrary to common perception, 90 per cent of older people live independently in mainstream housing,[15] with about six per cent in sheltered housing and four per cent in residential or similar settings. As noted earlier, most studies show that the majority of older people wish to remain living in their own homes and, in a related study by the Audit Commission,[16] key factors in achieving that aim of independent living included 'proximity to shops and services, accessibility, attractiveness and safety of the neighbourhood and attachment to area'.

A key question is whether the current housing stock and built environment is designed to enable the independent living aspirations of an ageing population. Do we have a built environment that supports inclusivity or gives rise to greater social exclusion in older age? And what are the lessons for new-build and regeneration?

Your place places you

Walk around any city, town or village and you will see housing inequality. Across the spectrum of housing, from the extremes of the homeless person on the street to the multi-million-pound country home or urban penthouse, housing is clearly not 'equal' at any age. There are deep divisions in Britain in terms of wealth, and given that housing is inextricably linked with financial status, these major social divides are reflected in people's housing situations. A person's home is the most visible outward symbol of their wealth and social status, with the term 'getting on the housing ladder' indicating a culture based to a significant degree on measuring success in life by progressive property acquisition. Thus, post-retirement, when social status is already being eroded as a consequence of no longer being in employment (as highlighted in Baroness Neuberger's chapter, Chapter Five), the status that housing confers can become even more important.

Your biggest asset?

Housing is about so much more than shelter from the elements. It has also become increasingly linked to financial investment, asset-based welfare and pensions provision.[17] The nation has become largely divided in terms of tenure. The transfer of advantage or disadvantage across the generations has been seen by the current government as being closely linked to home ownership.[18] Yet there still remains a basic human need for a roof over one's head, so the politics and policies that relate to housing, welfare and inequality are complex and challenging. This becomes even more the case in older age when housing and access to social care become intertwined; the vexed issue of home-owners using their home equity to pay care home fees is a case in point.

Policy and pronouncements

Britain has a mixed housing economy. The state does not determine where and how people are housed but offers some level of safety–net and financial help to those who are disadvantaged. While the British welfare state confers legal rights to education, healthcare and welfare benefits, it has never taken the step of making it the right of every citizen to be provided with a decent home. Successive governments have referred to giving people housing 'opportunities' to either rent or buy property, with the role of the state increasingly defined as an enabler rather than direct provider.

In a recent major housing policy document,[19] the then Housing Minister, Yvette Cooper MP, stated: 'The Government believes that everyone deserves a place they can be proud to call home, at a price they can afford.' The Prime Minister, Gordon Brown, in his foreword to the government's housing strategy for an ageing society,[20] declared: 'When I became Prime Minister I made giving everyone the chance to buy or rent a decent, affordable home one of my top priorities.'

In terms of age and inequality debates, the main focus has also been access to 'housing choice' and 'housing opportunity'. Equal treatment in the provision of housing-related services is highlighted, alongside design, planning and construction standards that result in greater equality of physical accessibility of place and space. Yet inequality in the treatment of older people compared with younger people with regard to many aspects of housing remains. Examples are described in the brochure *Age equality in housing*,[21] which concluded:

> In all of these examples, the options offered to older people are not what they want. Those involved in planning or providing housing are making false assumptions about older people, their needs, and the way they choose to live their lives. The result? Older people are devalued, ignored, dismissed or badly served.

As my co-author Julia Neuberger puts it elsewhere,[22] older people's future lives are determined on a miserably narrow range of choices when it comes to housing options.

The state's offer

The main areas of housing-related state input for older people are, at present:

- a housing safety-net for some disadvantaged groups, for example: state funding for social rented housing; for older people this has often meant specialist housing such as sheltered or extra-care housing;
- financial help with some housing-related costs; older people are key beneficiaries of Housing Benefit (for rental costs), Supporting People funding (for support services) and Disabled Facilities Grants (for home adaptations);
- setting minimum standards: for example, Building Regulations, Decent Homes Standards and planning controls, which determine, to some degree, the quality and location of homes across tenures; older people have been beneficiaries of the social rented Decent Homes programme to improve homes (even though older people in private housing remain the most likely to live in non-decent homes).

In these turbulent times, when housing is inextricably linked to the economic downturn, when the rules are being re-written with regard to the rights and responsibilities of the individual and the state in connection with all of the above areas, and when legislation is planned to outlaw age discrimination, it is timely to consider the key policy trends and issues that should inform the debates about housing, ageing and inequalities.

Much done, much more to do

Great strides have been taken during the past 50 years to improve the UK housing stock. Most people, including most older people, are now relatively well housed. However, there are still significant problems with the quality of the stock and its connection to age and social disadvantage (explored further in the Decent Homes section later). There are important issues to be addressed with regard to design suitability for an ageing population and inequalities in older people's housing situations.

Housing the demographic bulge

Figure 4.1: Population: by gender and age, mid-2007

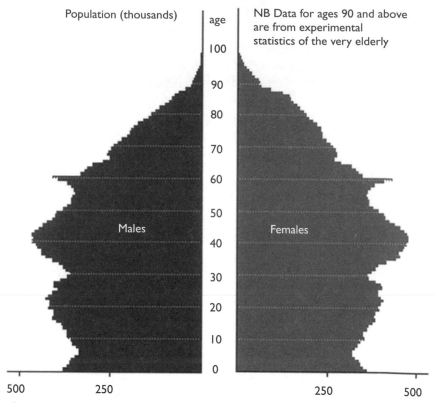

Source: www.statistics.gov.uk/cci/nugget.asp?ID=6

Much of the UK housing stock and infrastructure was built before the end of the Second World War: 40 per cent of homes were built before 1945, 19 per cent before 1919.[23] At this time the age profile of the population was very different: a pyramid with large numbers of children at the bottom and small numbers of older people at the pinnacle. Now, as Figure 4.1 above shows, that population shape is more like a barrel, with the post-war baby-boomers in the bulging middle and a decreasing younger population.

Matching politics and supply to demand and society

Despite such radical population change, the frame of reference for most mainstream home-building has been and remains the archetypal 'family house' for two adults and two children; 63 per cent of homes have three bedrooms or more, 27 per cent have two bedrooms, 10 per cent one bedroom.[24] Yet today 29 per cent of all households are single persons, 35 per cent are couples with no dependent children and only 29 per cent of households consist of families with children.

The highest rate of growth is in the number of single-person households, increasing by 30 per cent between 1990 and 2000.[25] Nearly half of all single householders (3.1 million) are pensioners, almost three quarters of whom are older women (2.4 million).[26] Two of the main factors driving this growth are ageing and changing family structures – for example, following divorce – and both remain on an upward trend.

So, are homes being built that address population ageing? It would seem not. The most notable recent building trend has been towards building urban centre flats. While partly a response to the rise of single households, this phenomenon has largely been driven by planning directives on higher density, rising land values and the boom in 'buy to invest'. In 2007–8, 48 per cent of new units of accommodation completed were flats.[27]

In contrast, the highest-profile housing problems are homeless families and associated local authority waiting lists. Consequently the 'homes for families' model remains dominant in current housing policy, particularly within the social rented sector. With the ongoing low rate of housing completions there will continue to be a mismatch between the supply of housing and the age profile of the population for the foreseeable future. This is likely to further exacerbate housing inequalities in older age in a number of ways, including a growing pressure on older tenants to move out of 'family housing' to make way for younger generations.

Ownership: not the magic wand

After ageing, one of the most radical social changes of the past half-century has been the shift into owner-occupation, primarily among lower-income groups. Rising from 50 per cent owner-occupation in 1970 to nearly 70 per cent today, and peaking at 84 per cent for the rural 'close-to-retirement' sub-group, this is a social change with specific implications for an ageing population. Two of the main drivers of this change were increased access to mortgages for lower-income groups combined with the Right to Buy initiative of the 1980s, whereby social rented tenants could buy their homes at a discounted rate.

Today there are as many low-income home-owners as low-income tenants. One of the reasons that this is of particular relevance to age and inequalities is the emerging problem of low-income home-owners retiring on low pensions and being unable to afford ongoing home repair and maintenance costs. The policy response to this conundrum was an expectation of increased use of equity release, with lower-income home-owners cashing in on the escalating value of their property. However, not only did equity release prove less popular than had been hoped, when the housing market went into crisis and property prices fell, it became an even less attractive option to many older people. The perceived unfairness and inequality of help from the welfare state for low-income home-owners *versus* tenants is a growing issue.

This inequity is illustrated by the case of two brothers, both in their 70s and living on the same ex-council estate. Let us call them Bill and Phil.

Bill

Bill worked as a garage fitter. He had been on a low income all his life and was now living on a state pension, Pension Credit and Council Tax benefit, the latter reduced because he has some moderate savings. He bought his home under the Right to Buy scheme and always did the repair and maintenance work himself. Reduced mobility means that he can no longer do this work and he faces problems with the cost of repairs. The house has draughty old windows and doors, defective electrical wiring, a sub-standard kitchen and bathroom, with poor thermal and heating standards. The value of the home is low and would not be enough to purchase a unit in the local retirement housing development.

Phil

Phil worked on and off during his earlier life as a casual labourer on building sites. He has remained a tenant on the same estate as Bill and lives on a state pension and Pension Credit; he also receives full Housing Benefit and Council Tax benefit. His house has undergone major renovation through the Decent Homes programme, including installation of a new bathroom and kitchen, double glazing, central heating, new wiring and roof. He is warm and comfortable in his home and happy to live there knowing that should his health and mobility deteriorate he would have a good chance of being able to move into one of the new extra-care housing schemes that have been built on the estate by a housing association.

Are we making headway?

Some policy responses are starting to emerge that deal with this growing area of inequality. Social lending supported by local authorities, such as interest-free or low-interest loans to pay for essential improvements, with a charge placed on the property repayable on sale, is growing, but again is likely to be affected by the economic downturn. An important initiative is increasing access to low-cost small repairs and minor adaptations. The government has provided funding for local authorities to expand the network of handyperson services, with a view to mainstreaming such provision by 2011.

One enabling strategy is the 'staircasing-out' of home ownership, whereby the older home-owner is able to release equity by selling stakes in their home to a housing association, so that they can then part-own/part-rent their home. Modelled on the subsidised 'staircasing-in' shared ownership schemes whereby occupants buy an increasing share in the home, this opportunity has been debated for a number of years, but with little action to date. Shared ownership in mixed-tenure extra-care and specialist housing schemes can also help to create more equal access for low-equity home-owners and is increasing, although the affordability of service charges for lower-income pensioners does need to be considered.

Homes fit for heroes? The Decent Homes Standard

Older people, particularly those over 75, are more likely than most younger age groups to live in non-decent homes, with the vast majority of those homes located in the private sector. Living in the same home for more than 25 years, being a single older woman or a BME elder – all are linked to increased likelihood of living in a non-decent home. The worst-housed group are private tenants, where 45 per cent of homes are non-decent.

The Decent Homes Standard[28] was introduced in 2000 alongside targets to bring all social rented housing up to the standard by 2010. In 2002 impetus to improve the private stock was added by the Public Service Agreement (PSA) target 7 to bring all social housing into decent condition by 2010, 'with most of the improvement taking place in deprived areas, and increase the proportion [to 70 per cent] of private housing in decent condition occupied by vulnerable groups'. Major investment in the improvement of social rented housing has since taken place. As the occupants of 34 per cent of all social rented housing, older people have gained significantly in terms of improved housing standards.[29]

Improvement in the private stock has been slower, and with the ending of the Decent Homes PSA target in 2008 there are no signs that this will improve. While bringing all social rented housing up to the Decent Homes Standard remains a national indicator in Local Area Agreements, there are now no national indicators or targets relating to the private sector and decent homes. There were an estimated 7.7 million non-decent homes (36 per cent of the stock) in 2007, the majority of which (5.3 million) were owner-occupied. Housing association stock is the least likely to be non-decent (26 per cent) and private rented accommodation most likely (45 per cent).

Lower state investment, higher costs

Over the past 25 years state expenditure on improvements to private sector stock has fallen, from £1,040 million in 1983/4 to £266 million 23 years later in 2006/7.[30] During that time the cost of building has gone up by a factor of more than three, and house price inflation by a factor of 8.6. Over these decades there has been a significant change in national government policy concerning the responsibility of the lower-income home-owner for home repair and maintenance. From the major investment via renovation grants for unfit properties during the peak years of 1982 to 1996 (when mandatory repair grants ended), there was a policy position that included a role for the state in financially supporting lower-income home-owners to improve properties. Older people were significant beneficiaries of this system, particularly following the creation of Minor Works Grants. There is now a more general expectation that home-owners should borrow commercially to meet repair and renovation costs, in the case of older people usually via equity release.

Rates of equity release take-up could be further reduced by the recession, with potential implications for the decline in housing quality. Given the impact of poor housing on older people's health and the consequent costs to the NHS, it makes economic sense to continue to offer some degree of financial help with essential repairs, especially for those most at risk, either via supported lending or expansion of the scope of the low-cost handyperson schemes. As unemployment rates rise, there is clear potential for training and employment initiatives linked to social gain.

Special housing for older people: designing-in inequality?

Although the vast majority of older people (90 per cent) live in general housing, the specialist sector still has an important role, particularly for specific vulnerable groups of older people – for example, those with intensive care needs, those with dementia, learning disabilities and more generally those over 80, who are the majority occupants of supported housing.[31]

The building of 'specialist' housing for older people has a chequered history with regard to treating older people equally compared with other age groups. An analysis of architecture and later-life living arrangements undertaken by Julienne Hanson[32] concluded that:

> Despite the recent emergence of new forms of sheltered and retirement housing in both the public and private sectors, such as extra-care housing and assisted living, a relatively uniform and formulaic design stereotype has dominated ... for about the last 50 years.

She demonstrates how much specialist housing is rooted in an 'almshouse stereotype', described by Fisk[33] as 'the physical expression of a benevolent paternalism'. Hanson concludes that this has exerted a disproportionate effect on the architecture of housing for older people, including design features that express the 'neediness' of the older person and the benevolence of the provider.

More years, less space

Much of today's sheltered housing stock was built during the 1960s, 1970s and 1980s, largely by the social rented sector, and significantly fuelled by a drive to get older people who were defined as 'under-occupying' to move out of family housing.[34] It was a low-cost, high-density initiative, building to very low space and design standards – even today, 25 per cent of sheltered housing units are bedsits. As a consequence, much of this stock has limited scope for adaptation as the mobility and function of older occupants decline.

As noted at the start of this chapter, housing is closely linked to social status and the amount of living space a person has is also closely connected to this. Space standards, particularly in the social rented sector, both in general new-build and in older people's housing, are a contentious issue. The Commission for Architecture and the Built Environment (CABE) and others are calling for improvement in the current situation where England is building homes with the lowest space standards in Europe. This issue of space is closely linked to unequal treatment on the grounds of age, and is highlighted in consultation with older people on housing aspiration.[35]

Hanson found that sheltered housing for older people is smaller than the equivalent provision for younger single people.[36] A typical 1970s bedsit has a net floor area of only 23.7m², while an early-1990s one-bed flat has 40.25m². The size of today's typical extra-care one-bed flat has increased only slightly, at 47.87m².

> 'I wonder why it is that they think because you are older you only need enough space to stand up, lie down and sit to eat? That's the impression it gives me!... And therefore the space is very confined, very small. The ceilings are low, the rooms are small, the kitchen – you couldn't swing a cat in it. Because you don't cook any more, do you, and you never entertain! So what do you want a kitchen for? You know, that's the thinking behind it!' (Mrs B, Engineering and Physical Sciences Research Council, EQUAL, 2001)

While the private specialist housing sector is segmented in such a way as to offer a wider range of options, with some schemes having much higher design and space standards (averaging 60m²),[37] those at the lower end of the market are smaller and some do not meet the Lifetime Homes Standards noted later.

With age, people spend an increasing amount of time at home, rising from an average of 80 per cent at age 65 to 90 per cent for those aged 85 and over.[38] So the quality and suitability of the home is a major factor in general health and emotional well-being. In addition, the acquisition of possessions over a lifetime means that the availability of space for furniture, storage of valued items and space for hobbies and activities are important in designing housing for older age, which is not currently catered for in most specialist housing.

A radical rethink of specialist housing for older people that does not result in greater inequality, stigmatisation or exclusion is overdue. The government's plans for an innovation panel to undertake this is therefore a welcome step.[39] What will be even more important is the subsequent implementation.

Older people are still people

'We are as varied and different when we are older as when we are younger' is the mantra of the active older age lobby, which rightly rails against the stereotyping of older people in all aspects of daily life. If, as seems to be the current trend, older age is defined as beginning at 50, it will last for half a lifetime for the increasing number of people who reach 100. Hence, there is going to be a very wide spectrum of housing experience, need and aspiration over some four to five decades, and with a wide variety of situations with regard to health and disability.

Better housing, better health

Tackling health inequalities has been a government policy priority for a number of years.[40] Many of the common chronic health conditions linked to early death and inequality, especially for older people, have a causal link to housing. These include heart disease, stroke, mental health, respiratory conditions, arthritis and rheumatism.[41] Hence, addressing the issue of a better built environment and housing design for an ageing population is closely connected with addressing health inequality.

Unequal ageing: daily living

Many older people remain fit and active well into older age. A very significant minority decline in health and mobility. While years have been added to life, most of these are not yet healthy years, and this is particularly the case for lower-income groups. Not only is there a significant social inequality in life expectancy, but also in healthy life expectancy. A number of studies published as part of the English Longitudinal Study of Ageing[42] have quantified some of the links between health, age and inequality. It was found that one in five of those aged 50 and over, and two in five of those aged 80 and over, reported difficulties with one or more aspects of basic self-care – such as washing and dressing – and mobility.

Other studies demonstrated a 'social gradient' in health: the lower a person's social position, the greater the level of ill health and loss of physical function.[43] There is a remarkably large geographical variation for disability-free life expectancy. For men there is an 18-year difference between the worst area (Easington) and the best (Hart), while for women the difference is 16.4 years (Merthyr Tydfil *versus* Elmbridge).[44]

One very immediate housing consequence of such inequalities is that poorer older people are more likely to need adaptations to their homes in order to live independently.[45] It is estimated[46] that the number of disabled older people in England will double, from 2.3 million in 2002 to 4.6 million by 2041. Access to help with home adaptation is of itself a matter of significant inequality, not only as a result of wealth but also geographical location, with variable local availability of Disabled Facilities Grants or discretionary help offered by housing authorities and social services.[47]

In the report on the 2006/7 Survey of English Housing,[48] Communities and Local Government (CLG) reports that six million households include an occupant with a disability or serious medical condition. Of these, 1.4 million individuals reported having a medical condition or disability that resulted in them requiring specially adapted accommodation. Eighty-five per cent were over 45 and about half lived in owner-occupied accommodation. Seventy-eight per cent reported that they lived in a home that was 'suitable' for coping with the medical condition or disability. And older people were more likely than people with disabled children to report unsuitability. It is noteworthy that there has been a 60 per cent increase in five years in the number of over-85s who report a disability or serious medical condition.

Falls and housing

Falls are one of the major causes of death and health decline among older people,[49] and there is an established causal link between housing condition and falling.[50] The prevalence of poor or unsuitable housing conditions among disadvantaged older households can increase the risk of falls.[51]

In the UK an older person dies approximately every five hours as a result of a fall, and many more are injured and hospitalised.[52] Hip fractures alone cost £1.8 billion a year. The vast majority of falls take place in the older person's home where housing design, adaptation and other modifications (such as improved lighting)[53] have a proven impact on reducing falls. Many also occur in the wider neighbourhood. Here there is further potential to reduce the incidence of falls through simple measures such as dropped kerbs, level pavements, well-designed public seating and good street lighting.

In setting out his agenda for greater fairness in an ageing society at a Fabian Society lecture in 2009, Professor Alan Walker included tackling falls, as well as excess winter deaths, among his top priorities:

> It is difficult to speak of fairness while this scandal persists and, in more positive terms, it is a problem waiting to be fixed by an ambitious programme of Keynesian-style public works.[54]

Cold-related ill health

One of the greatest health inequalities between older people and the wider population is excess winter deaths. Between December 2007 and March 2008 there were an estimated 25,300 deaths in England and Wales, an increase of 1,000 from the previous winter.[55] A sharp rise in fuel prices and an exceptionally cold winter in 2008–9 are indicators that the numbers may have risen again as there is a close correlation between winter temperature and death rate. The gradient of increase in winter deaths in the UK is steeper than in colder countries, such as Scandinavia, which have better housing, so it is often argued that the thermal standard of properties in the UK is a significant causal factor.

There is now a growing impetus for the building of new homes to higher thermal efficiency standards via the Code for Sustainable Homes. Significant gains have been made in improving the thermal efficiency of the social rented housing stock through the Decent Homes programme, and the government has invested in Warm Front to provide targeted help with heating and insulation for disadvantaged households, with low-income pensioners the main beneficiaries. As a response to rising fuel prices, winter fuel payments for pensioners have also been increased.

However, despite these measures the government looks set to miss its target of ending fuel poverty. More drastic measures are needed. A systematic programme of retrofitting and more radical improvement to the existing stock is increasingly being argued for by a wide spectrum of organisations, including Age Concern and Help the Aged.

Incontinence: the silent exclusion

The incidence of incontinence increases significantly with age, with an estimated three to six million people across the UK affected by it.[56] This rarely mentioned problem is increasingly being recognised as having implications for the design of age-friendly homes and neighbourhoods. At home, easy access to a WC (that is, downstairs as well as upstairs) and accessible washing facilities (that is, related to provision of showers and adapted bathing facilities) are critical to dignity and personal hygiene. Outdoors, in the wider neighbourhood, the availability of public toilets has a major impact on many older people's ability to get out and about. There is an increasingly vociferous campaign emerging to increase provision.[57] Local authorities should not merely have a power to provide public toilets. It should be a duty.

Emerging solutions: Lifetime Homes, Lifetime Neighbourhoods

A fundamental element of the current policy response to population ageing and the equalities agenda is a stated commitment to creating inclusive homes and neighbourhoods that are designed to meet people's needs better, whatever their age or ability.

The Joseph Rowntree Foundation and Habinteg Housing have pioneered the concept of Lifetime Homes for nearly two decades.[58] It is based on a set of design features that create a high-quality home environment which enables residents to live well in that home for as long as possible, regardless of their physical abilities. The standard identifies a set of key design criteria that, if planned from the outset, can be incorporated into all new mainstream housing. An important part of the philosophy behind Lifetime Homes is the creation of inclusive buildings, including homes, which enable equal access to mainstream housing by disabled people so that they are able to visit friends and relatives and take an active part in society, rather than being confined to an 'adapted box'.

The national strategy: a stride forward?

The government has made a commitment to the inclusion of Lifetime Homes Standards into all new social rented housing by 2011 and an aspiration to see all housing built, including all private housing, to Lifetime Homes Standards by 2013. Application of the standard is being reviewed in 2010 and if adequate progress is not being made, regulation will be considered to enforce implementation. This is an important step in terms of age equality, disability, housing and access.

Following on from the idea of creating accessible housing that is inclusive to all is the concept of the 'lifetime neighbourhood'. The discussion paper *Towards lifetime neighbourhoods: Designing sustainable communities for all*, published jointly by CLG and the International Longevity Centre UK (ILCUK),[59] uses the following definition:

> Lifetime neighbourhoods are those which offer everyone the best possible chance of health, well-being, and social, economic and civic engagement regardless of age. They provide the built environment, infrastructure, housing, services and shared social space that allow us to pursue our own ambitions for a high quality of life. They do not exclude us as we age, nor as we become frail or disabled.

This report covered many of the themes included in the World Health Organization's *Global age-friendly cities: A guide*.[60] In its housing strategy for an ageing society in England, the government[61] made a commitment to encouraging the development of lifetime neighbourhoods. The strategy noted that as people get older they spend more of their time at or close to home and proximity/accessibility of basic services and facilities was therefore even more important. It also demonstrated how problems in accessing amenities increased with age.

Putting it all together: *Towards common ground*

Help the Aged has since published a manifesto for lifetime neighbourhoods, *Towards common ground*, proposing 10 components that should be the minimum requirement for inclusive neighbourhoods and communities.[62] These cover a range of issues such as accessible public transport, toilets, seating, quality of pavements, open spaces, places to meet and inclusion of older people in local decision-making.

Figure 4.1: Towards common ground

Source: Help the Aged (2008) *Towards common ground*, London: Help the Aged.

The extent to which these fundamental changes to the built environment will be incorporated into everyday planning, into regeneration schemes and new-build programmes is still uncertain as there are a limited number of hard targets and policy drivers. However, it is important that a process has at least started to address inequality through better design of place and space.

The current crisis in the building industry, and the consequent major reduction in the building of new homes, provides an opportunity to drive up the standards in future new homes when building starts to take off again, thereby addressing demographic change and the range of related issues highlighted earlier.

Creating out of crisis: some emerging policy debates

Until the recession began to bite, home ownership would probably have been seen by most people as a positive social development, a welcome opportunity for low-income groups to move into the world of home ownership, with all the choices of home location and potential for wealth gain that this had come to represent. For an ageing population, this increased housing wealth was expected to support old age in a variety of ways, from supplementing pensions to offering greater housing options, potential release of equity through downsizing, and cascading of wealth across the generations. Asset-based welfare would mean that the role of the state in terms of housing and older age would decline, reducing costs to the Treasury. The downside was a growing gulf between renters and owners as social renting, and some private renting, became even more of a 'tenure of last resort', resulting in even greater social inequalities for people in older age.

The reality was much more complex. Disadvantage now straddles tenure with some low-equity/low-income older home-owners having even fewer housing options and living in worse housing than older social rented housing tenants. The time is now ripe to look again at the systems of housing-related support for all low-income older people across tenure. In the face of rising repossessions the government is rapidly revising its approach to financial assistance for home-owners, introducing earlier help for people with mortgages and shared-ownership rescue packages. This may ultimately result in a more comprehensive examination of the inequalities in the current systems of financial help for low-income older home-owners as, for example, commercial equity release can no longer be expected to provide the answer to all problems of disrepair and income shortfall.

There is an interconnection with the current fundamental policy debate about who pays for social care in older age, where moving towards a sharing of responsibility between the individual and the state is being seriously considered instead of the current 'all or nothing' situation. A similar level of public discussion is needed in terms of general housing in older age.

One of the recurring themes in the social housing sector that may impact on older tenants is the debate about security of tenure. In the face of a shortage of social rented homes, periodic reassessment of a tenant's 'need' for their social rented home is being seriously considered by both major political parties and the housing regulators. Given the often expressed concerns among social rented housing providers about older people 'under-occupying' family homes, this is a trend that should be of concern to the older people's sector. As noted earlier, a home is far more than bricks and mortar. Feeling secure in one's home is key to emotional health.

The heart of the matter

But perhaps even more fundamental to all of these specific debates concerning older people, housing and inequality is an underlying but unspoken assumption that older people are not really valuable to society. This deep-rooted, rarely acknowledged and frequently denied belief underpins many of the specific issues highlighted earlier. Only when the worlds of architecture, design, planning and housing have understood and embraced the concept of positive ageing are we likely to see the creation of truly age-inclusive homes and neighbourhoods.

Five things we can do now

1. Build all new homes to Lifetime Homes Standards as a minimum design standard across all tenures; apply them to substantial improvement of current stock.
2. The key national players should work together to agree Lifetime Neighbourhoods Standards based on the development work already done, as described in *Age-friendly cities* and *Towards common ground*.
3. Create a legal right to housing-related support such as rapid-response adaptations and essential minor repairs.
4. Invest in the development and building of new types of housing such as co-housing and Community Land Trusts.
5. Oblige all plans for homes and neighbourhoods to have regard to demographic change and ageing.

Notes

[1] WHO (World Health Organization) (2008) *Closing the gap in a generation: Health equity through action on the social determinants of health*, Final report of the commission on social determinants of health, Geneva: WHO.

[2] English House Conditions Survey 2008.

[3] Blackman, T. (2005) *Housing risks and health inequalities in housing*, London: Department of Health Housing LIN.

[4] Clough, R., Leamy, M. and Bright, L. (2003) *Homing in on housing*, Lancaster: ESR.

[5] Clough, R. (ed) (2004) *Housing decisions in later life*, Basingstoke: Palgrave Macmillan.

[6] Heywood, F., Oldman, C. and Means, R. (2002) *Housing and home in later life*, Milton Keynes: Open University Press.

[7] CLG (Communities and Local Government) (2008) *Housing choices and aspirations of older people: Research from the New Horizons Programme*, London: CLG; Clough, R., Leamy, M. and Bright, L. (2003) *Homing in on housing*, Lancaster: ESR; Tinker, A., Askham, J., Hancock, J. et al (2001) *Eighty-five not out: A study of people aged 85 and over at home*, Oxfordshire: Anchor Trust.

[8] CLG (Communities and Local Government) (2008) *Lifetime homes, lifetime neighbourhoods: A national strategy for housing in an ageing society*, London: CLG.

[9] BGOP (Better Government for Older People) (2000) *All our futures*, London: BGOP.

[10] Government Actuary Department, 2006-based population projections (www.gad.gov.uk).

[11] CLG (Communities and Local Government) Survey of English Housing Data, CLG (annual).

[12] Ibid.

[13] Care & Repair England (2008) *A survey of regional housing strategies and regional spatial strategies*, Nottingham: Care & Repair England.

[14] Age Concern (2004) *Now you see me, now you don't: How are older citizens being included in regeneration?*, London: Age Concern.

[15] CLG (Communities and Local Government) Survey of English Housing Data, CLG (annual).

[16] Audit Commission (2004) *Older people: A changing approach: Independence and well-being*, London: Audit Commission.

[17] Maxwell, D. and Sodha, S. (2006) *Housing wealth: First timers to old timers*, London: IPPR.

[18] Fabian Society 'Next decade' lectures by Housing Ministers Ruth Kelly and Yvette Cooper, 2007–8.

[19] CLG (Communities and Local Government) (2007) *Homes for the future: More affordable, more sustainable*, Green Paper, London: CLG.

[20] CLG (Communities and Local Government) (2008) *Lifetime homes, lifetime neighbourhoods: A national strategy for housing in an ageing society*, London: CLG.

[21] HOPDEV (Housing and Older People Development Group) (2006) *Age equality in housing: A guide to tackling age discrimination for housing providers, commissioners, planners and builders*, London: HOPDEV (http://hopdev. housingcare.org/downloads/kbase/age-equality-leaflet.pdf).

[22] Neuberger, J. (2008) *Not dead yet: A manifesto for old age*, London: HarperCollins.

[23] CLG (Communities and Local Government) (2008) *Housing in England 2006/7*, London: CLG.

[24] Ibid.

[25] Census 2001 data, Office for National Statistics website (www.ons.gov. uk).

[26] Ibid.

[27] CLG (Communities and Local Government) (2009) 'Live tables on house building', London: CLG (www.communities.gov.uk/documents/housing/ xls/table254.xls).

[28] ODPM (Office of the Deputy Prime Minister) (2006) *A decent home: Definition and guidance for implementation*, London: ODPM.

[29] The Housing Corporation (2008) *Investing for lifetimes*, London: The Housing Corporation.

[30] The figure for 1983/4 is from Wilcox, S. (2001) *Housing finance review 1999–2000*, York/Coventry: Joseph Rowntree Foundation/Chartered Institute of Housing. The figure for 2006/7 is from CLG (Communities and Local Government) (2008) *Housing statistics*, London: CLG.

[31] CLG (Communities and Local Government) (2008) *Lifetime homes, lifetime neighbourhoods: A national strategy for housing in an ageing society*, London: CLG.

[32] Sumner, K. (ed) (2002) *Our homes, our lives*, London: The Housing Corporation and Centre for Policy on Ageing.

[33] Fisk, M. (1999) *Our future home: Housing and the inclusion of older people in 2025*, London: Help the Aged.

[34] Hanson, J., Kellaher, L. and Rowlands, M. (2001) *Profiling the housing stock for older people: The transition from domesticity to caring*, Final report of EPSRC EQUAL Research, London: University College, London.

[35] HOPDEV (Housing and Older People Development Group) (2006) *Key messages from older people*, London: HOPDEV.

[36] Hanson, J., Kellaher, L. and Rowlands, M. (2001) *Profiling the housing stock for older people: The transition from domesticity to caring*, Final report of EPSRC EQUAL Research, London: University College, London.

[37] Ibid.

[38] Adams, S. and White, K. (2006) *Older people, decent homes and fuel poverty*, London: Help the Aged.

[39] CLG (Communities and Local Government) (2008) *Lifetime homes, lifetime neighbourhoods: A national strategy for housing in an ageing society*, London: CLG.

[40] DH (Department of Health) (2002) *Tackling health inequalities: Summary of the cross-cutting review*, London: DH.

[41] Blackman, T. (2005) *Housing risks and health inequalities in housing*, London: Department of Health Housing LIN.

[42] IFS (Institute for Fiscal Studies) (2002 onwards) *English Longitudinal Study of Ageing*, London: IFS.

[43] Ibid.

[44] Office for National Statistics website (www.ons.gov.uk).

[45] OPDM (Office of the Deputy Prime Minister) (2005) *Reviewing the Disabled Facilities Grant*, London: ODPM.

[46] CLG (Communities and Local Government) (2008) *Lifetime homes, lifetime neighbourhoods: A national strategy for housing in an ageing society*, London: CLG.

[47] OPDM (Office of the Deputy Prime Minister) (2005) *Reviewing the Disabled Facilities Grant*, London: ODPM.

[48] CLG (Communities and Local Government) (2008) *Housing in England 2006/7*, London: CLG.

[49] WHO (World Health Organization) (2007) *Global report on falls prevention in older age*, Geneva: WHO.

[50] Heywood, F. (2006) *Better outcomes, lower costs: Implications for health and social care budgets of investment in housing adaptation, improvements and equipment: A review of evidence*, London: Department for Work and Pensions (commissioned by the Office for Disability Issues).

[51] ODPM (Office of the Deputy Prime Minister) (2003) *Statistical evidence to support the housing health and safety rating system: Volume II – Summary of results*, Coventry and London: University of Warwick, London School of Hygiene and Tropical Medicine, ODPM.

[52] DTI (Department for Trade and Industry) (2002) *Home accident surveillance system including leisure activities: 24th (final) annual report*, London: DTI and RoSPA, various (www.rospa.com/homesafety/advice/index.htm#old).

[53] Heywood, F. (2006) *Better outcomes, lower costs: Implications for health and social care budgets of investment in housing adaptation, improvements and equipment: A review of evidence*, London: Department for Work and Pensions (commissioned by The Office for Disability Issues).

[54] Walker, A. (2009) 'Fairness in an ageing society' (http://fabians.org.uk/index2.php?option=com_content&do_pdf=1&id=773).

[55] Brock, B. (2008) 'Excess winter mortality in England and Wales, 2007/8 (provisional) and 2006/7 (final)', *Health Statistics Quarterly*, vol 40, Winter, Office for National Statistics, The Stationery Office.

[56] Help the Aged (2008) *Towards common ground*, London: Help the Aged.

[57] Neuberger, J. (2008) *Not dead yet: A manifesto for old age*, London: HarperCollins.

[58] www.lifetimehomes.org.uk/

[59] CLG (Communities and Local Government) and ILCUK (International Longevity Centre UK) (2007) *Towards lifetime neighbourhoods: Designing sustainable communities for all*, London: CLG and ILCUK.

[60] WHO (World Health Organization) (2007) *Global age-friendly cities: A guide*, Geneva: WHO.

[61] CLG (Communities and Local Government) (2008) *Lifetime homes, lifetime neighbourhoods: A national strategy for housing in an ageing society*, London: CLG.

[62] Help the Aged (2008) *Towards common ground*, London: Help the Aged.

FIVE

What does it mean to be old?

Baroness Julia Neuberger

- Seventy-five per cent of older people surveyed think the views of their age group are ignored by the media.[1]
- The story of the abuse of the child Victoria Climbié attracted over 300 mentions in the press; the equally horrific experiences of 78-year-old Margaret Panting received just five.[2]
- Twenty-seven per cent of people surveyed thought that people aged over 70 are viewed with pity.[3]

Ageism ... in our bloodstream

We live in an inherently ageist society – ageism is well recognised and it is the most commonly experienced form of discrimination.[4] Whether it is the lack of provision of automatic call and recall for breast cancer screening for women over 73 (the implication is that they are no longer part of the working and therefore 'useful' population, so their lives do not matter as much as those of younger women), or the assumption that it is perfectly acceptable to play blaring rock music on the radio to a room full of frail older people in a care home because the staff like it, without consideration for what the residents like, discrimination against older people, in almost all aspects of their lives, is profound and disabling. And it devalues those who display that level of ignorance and unfair discrimination as much as it impacts with negative effect on the older people who experience it.

'Successful' ageing ...

Age discrimination is widespread, but it does not necessarily affect all older people. There are those older people – usually the very old – who become in some way national treasures. Diana Athill, enjoying a renaissance in popularity as a writer in her 90s with her book *Somewhere towards the end*, is a case in point, winning the biography category of the Costa book awards in January 2009.[5] Frances Partridge, the last of the Bloomsbury Group, who died at 103 in 2004, really achieved fame in her later years with her biography of Julia Strachey and her five volumes of diaries, and was another 'national treasure'. But these were and are exceptional women, though by no means alone.

Those who live into a healthy and sufficiently wealthy older age, with activities for the mind and the capacity to feel needed, are not necessarily discriminated against as much as those whose bodies play them up more or whose minds begin to go. Nor are the wealthy as discriminated against as those whose financial resources are so limited that they are dependent on social services for much of the help that they need – at which point being assessed by someone else, a so-called expert, as to what would be useful and necessary, takes over from making personal choices. Indeed, those who are by virtue of their health or financial or other situation vulnerable are also those who are also the most discriminated against, whether by being allowed only one bath a week when unable to bathe or shower themselves, or by being required to receive a 'one-size-fits-all' service in terms of carers or indeed meals on wheels.

... or expensive burdens?

Older people are depicted on road signs as bent over, leaning on sticks. Despite the fact that some older people are bent and/or may use a walking stick, the caricature is a cruel one. Older people are seen as a cost to society: if that were not so, how could it be possible to split up a very old couple, such as Richard and Beryl Driscoll, who were separated for seven months at the age of 89 after 65 years of marriage, because Gloucestershire Social Services refused to pay for Mrs Driscoll to live in a care home alongside her frailer husband, even though she was blind?[6]

And worst of all is forced retirement from work and sometimes even from volunteering, on the basis that older people have no place in our workplace or in our wider society. This is not only foolish in emotional terms, and cruel, leaving many older people feeling useless, but counterproductive in terms of the cost to society at large – with an ageing population and increasing life expectancy, it makes no sense to retire at 60 or 65. Yet by the time we reach that age, we are described as 'wrinklies', at best, and as 'past it' or past our 'sell-by date'.

Even the best of voluntary organisations, which organise all kinds of volunteering for people of all ages and backgrounds, often argue that getting insurance cover for their older volunteers is so expensive or difficult it simply is 'not worth it'. But the question has to be: to whom is it not worth it? Is it simply inconceivable to the younger people running such organisations that older people still have a serious contribution to make? Is it beyond the wit of younger men and women to see that older people need to be needed, as do all of us, and that carrying on as volunteers for as long as they are able is what keeps them alive and gives them meaning in their lives?

It is as if older people somehow become invisible in terms of emotional needs, and the result of that, alongside other forms of discrimination, means that our ageist stereotypes have a real impact on older people's lives, and limit their sphere of influence and activity.

Lone voices

Some older people, such as the writers mentioned above, and the new Voice of Older People, Dame Joan Bakewell, appointed in late 2008 by the government to speak out on older people's issues, or the writer Katharine Whitehorn, who was the guest on *Desert Island Discs* on BBC Radio 4 in 2008 after her autobiography, *Selective memory*, had been reprinted five times, have largely escaped being labelled as 'old', except by themselves, and have a different experience of ageing from those who are identified as old from 65–70 or so.

But talk to almost any older person about how difficult it is to go out without recourse to public toilets, and the realisation that many older people are simply trapped at home for fear of being 'caught short' strikes you forcibly. Or ask any older person about shopping, and most will tell you that the lack of availability of seats in shops makes shopping a very stressful experience – and an unpleasant one. Yet it is small physical changes, often associated with age, which lead to life being made more difficult, and the lack of provision by local authorities to accommodate those physical changes makes for loneliness and exclusion.

Health warnings on age

Add into that a growing number of (often relatively minor) ailments, with a health service that clearly discriminates against older people in how quickly it responds and the extent to which it regards older people as being worthy of repair, and you have a clear demonstration of how the public realm can lead to you being labelled old and thereby excluded from a whole variety of services you would have been offered had you been younger. That is as true in cardiology as in stroke, both serious, as in cholesterol testing and in attitudes to acute treatment, and it depends to a very large extent on the attitudes of the individual doctors and nurses concerned, brought up in, and accultured to, our National Health Service.[7]

Poor expectations, poorer life chances

But that is not all. Part of the problem here rests with the professional definitions of what successful ageing consists of. When Ann Bowling and Paul Dieppe carried out a huge literature review of what experts had said successful ageing was, they found that the experts left out of their long list a large number of extra lay definitions which older people themselves had listed – and older people ought to know, after all. These extra definitions included accomplishments, enjoyment of food, financial security, neighbourhood, physical appearance, productivity and contribution to life, a sense of humour, a sense of purpose, and a sense of spirituality. These are, after all, the categories that make anyone tick at any stage of their lives; but when professionals looked at successful ageing they were completely absent, replaced instead by such things as physical functioning, adaptability, coping and self-esteem.[8]

These age prejudices, professionalised in a lack of sensitivity to what older people, and people in general, really care about, and held by the wider public in a rather incoherent way – 'this older person is useless, yet I would not say that about my mother or father' – feed and exacerbate unequal experiences of ageing. And those who face other disadvantages, of poverty, for instance, or disability that is long-standing, tend to experience the losses of dignity and respect earlier – the marginalisation they have already experienced as a result of other factors, such as ethnicity, exacerbates and multiplies the problems they face.

Perceptions of age: others, not us

Discrimination against older people is based on prejudice – a view of what older people will and should be like. It may be a caricature of granny sitting by the fire knitting or grandpa gardening and chatting to his grandchild. It may be the hobbling older person who finds it hard to get around, or the older person who is hard of hearing, leading to younger people shouting rather than speaking more clearly. It may be a picture of older people as hideous, or worthless, or useless. All of these are born of prejudice that may not be universal, but is widely shared.

It comes, as all unfair discrimination does, from a sense that older people are different from us, are 'other' – and inherent in that conception of 'other' is a view that somehow we will never be like that, while in our heart of hearts we of course know that we too will become old, unless we die first. This makes age discrimination different in kind from the prejudices against people on the basis of ethnicity, gender or sexual orientation – we may or may not share the ethnicity, gender or sexual orientation, but we cannot escape our birth date. In the case of age, we will surely get there ourselves, and our lack of capacity to envisage our own older age is one of the factors that makes this particular form of discrimination so distressing. Yet older people are no longer 'other', and different from us. As we age, in most Western societies older people are 'most people'. They are us.

Blanket analysis

Yet despite the large numbers of older people and the wide diversity of the older population – just like the rest of the population – older people are still stereotyped as a single entity. In no other case would we categorise people within an age range of 40 years as being a coherent group, yet we talk of people from 60 to 100+ as 'older people' without differentiating, even between the older and younger old. We cannot rely on this phenomenon simply to fade out as people realise its absurdity. All the experience of other forms of discrimination suggests that that does not work, that society has to set itself goals to reach to root out age discrimination – and Parliament has to enact legislation to stamp it out, in just the same way as happened over race and gender. And even then it took a whole generation before people at large began to think that there was something seriously wrong with sex and race discrimination.

Benign prejudice

Yet prejudice on the basis of age, unlike some other prejudices such as those based on race or sexual orientation, is not always malign. Some of the most discriminatory terms, some of the most offensive caricatures, are said or drawn with a note of affection in the music. You hear, for instance, the expression 'doddery but dear'.[9] Others think the term 'wrinklies' is affectionate, while still others characterise themselves as 'old bags', or 'old gits' – self deprecating, perhaps, because that makes it easier to deal with others' negative stereotypes. Being a doddery old dear or a wrinkly is not necessarily seen as a 'bad' thing to be, although they are certainly not models to aspire to. Also, the lack of goals in terms of aspiration for age means that one cannot rationally aspire to be an older person, even though it may happen by default.

From respect to revulsion

Older people do not command respect. The biblical injunction to 'Honour your father and your mother' (Exodus 20:12) or 'you shall respect (hold in awe) your mother and your father' (Leviticus 19:3) is stated in the Ten Commandments and elsewhere precisely because, one might argue, it needs to be emphasised, not being instinctive.

Nevertheless, most early societies did look after their older people, and treated them with something akin to respect, however hard it may have been. In our 21st-century Western society, and most particularly in the UK, we have come to a stage where age has become more than something unattractive. It is now seen as somewhat repellent, which is presumably why care workers, in some of the notorious cases where older people have been severely neglected in hospital or nursing homes, have found it possible to treat people badly: they find them repellent simply because of their age, and of course because of their vulnerability and dependency as well. Inherent in that ignoring of older people's dignity and personhood is a belief that these people would be better off dead.

As hard evidence of this hard reality, we now know that abuse of older people is extremely widespread. Research funded by Comic Relief quantified the level of elder abuse *in the community alone* at some 342,400 cases at any one time, when the estimates included abuse by friends, neighbours and acquaintances. Further research is in hand to assess the probably even larger scale and scope of abuse in institutions.

The media are the message

That sense of old age being repulsive finds its voice in the depiction of older people as figures of fun and ridicule.[10] There are many examples from the media, such as older people in Disney movies, where research shows that 'while the majority of older characters are portrayed as positive characters, there is still a large percentage that is portrayed in a negative manner. These results help explain why children have negative feelings toward older people.'[11] Or there was the veteran political journalist John Sergeant on the hit reality TV show, *Strictly Come Dancing*,[12] who had to quit the show in November 2008 because there was a real risk of him winning as a result of the public vote – despite the attitude of the judges. Sergeant was ranked last by the judges for three weeks, only to be rescued by the public vote each time while more talented contestants were sent home. He was also roundly insulted along the way, at least in part because of his age, with one judge describing him as 'a dancing pig in Cuban heels'.

Too old to lead

'Old' has increasingly become an insult. If our politicians show their age, they are somehow giving away something shameful. That was memorably true with Sir Menzies Campbell as leader of the Liberal Democrats.[13]

'Welcome to the scrapheap!' Caricature can make a point with great power. The birthday card sent to newly 50-year-old MPs in 2003 as Tony Blair himself hit 50 struck a blow for age discrimination. But *The Guardian* cartoon about Menzies Campbell's leadership told an even sorrier story.

Source: Steve Bell for Help the Aged

Source: Steve Bell for *The Guardian*

But he was not alone. Vince Cable decided not to stand for the leadership of the Liberal Democrats in the wake of Menzies' departure when he himself was only a couple of years younger:

> I did seriously think about it, and I knew I could do it and would do it well, but the general consensus among colleagues was that because Ming Campbell was almost kicked to death because of his age they couldn't risk a candidate of the same generation. (Interview in *The Guardian*, 12 February 2008)

Yet in the US little attention was given, in the 2008 presidential campaign, to John McCain's age. Rather, the emphasis was on his state of health, given a previous history of melanoma, and his allowing the press to see his health records back in 2005 – perhaps a proxy for concern about his age. Arguably, attitudes to the age of politicians are less negative in the US than in the UK as are attitudes to older people generally.

Communicating respect

In November 2008, guidance sent round to nurses in new guidelines from the Nursing and Midwifery Council caused an outcry. Calling older patients 'dearie' or 'love' was ruled out as offensive, and nurses were told that they should speak 'courteously and respectfully' and use patients' preferred names. The document, *Guidance for the care of older people*, argues that effective communication is one of the most valuable skills that a nurse can have, and that poor communication can damage the relationship between a nurse and an older person.

But in radio and TV debate on the issue views were very mixed, with many listeners commenting that they rather liked being called 'dear' or 'duck' – and it was not the terms used, but the attitude of the person who used them, that mattered. Nevertheless, the fact is that enough older people find the term of endearment without the use of their full name undignified and lacking in respect. Meanwhile, in the US, the term 'elderspeak' has been invented, to characterise the demeaning speech, supposedly affectionate, which is used to and sometimes about older people.

A *New York Times* article looked at the issue from several angles:

> 'People think they're being nice', said Elvira Nagle, 83, of Dublin, California, 'but when I hear it, it raises my hackles.'

Now studies are finding that the insults can have health consequences, especially if people mutely accept the attitudes behind them, said Becca Levy, an associate professor of epidemiology and psychology at Yale University: 'Those little insults can lead to more negative images of aging. And those who have more negative images of aging have worse functional health over time, including lower rates of survival.' In a long-term survey of 660 people over age 50 in a small Ohio town, published in 2002, Dr Levy and her fellow researchers found that those who had positive perceptions of aging lived an average of 7.5 years longer, a bigger increase than that associated with exercising or not smoking. The findings held up even when the researchers controlled for differences in the participants' health conditions.... Despite such research, the worst offenders are often healthcare workers, said Kristine Williams, a nurse gerontologist and associate professor at the University of Kansas School of Nursing.[14]

Why age prejudice? Familiarity breeds respect

So why does this prejudice against older people still exist, particularly in an ageing society? One theory is that there is remarkably little contact between different groups in society, and particularly between old and young. It is well known that 'positive contact' (such as close, personal friendship) between members of different groups in society has been shown to reduce prejudice and discrimination. Conversely, lack of positive contact, or contact which is negative, can increase the likelihood of prejudice.

Age Concern Kent's research found that contact between age groups was age-restricted. More people of all ages had positive contact with younger people than older people (80 per cent overall having a friendship with someone under 30 compared to 67 per cent having a friendship with someone over 70).[15] And Janet Street-Porter, responding to a survey that showed that 90 per cent of the population thought older people should be cherished and 60 per cent thought older people enriched our cultural life, commented acidly: 'Oh really? If that is the case, how come we don't take the time and trouble to know any of these national treasures? Half of those under 24 who were surveyed didn't know anyone over 70, and *vice versa*. If older people are so supersonic, how come the country is full of homes where ageing relatives have been parked out of sight?'[16]

Denying death

There is also the distinct possibility that part of the negative attitude to older people lies in a particular fear. Ernest Becker argued in his Pulitzer Prize-winning work, *The denial of death*, published in 1973, that human civilisation is ultimately an elaborate, symbolic defence mechanism against the knowledge of our mortality. That in turn acts as the emotional and intellectual response to our basic survival mechanism. That way, 'older people are a constant uncomfortable reminder to the young of the inevitability of death.... In order for the cultural worldview of death denial to be maintained, older people are pushed from view both physically and psychologically. Research shows that when people's death anxiety is raised they show more ageist attitudes.'[17]

If the numbers of older people are increasing, then perhaps the reminder of mortality is ever-present; even though people are living longer, therefore death is further away, the reality is that they are also living frailer, and more vulnerable lives, at the end – and that may also be a cause of fear for younger people. But it is not only about the fear of mortality. In recent years, with an ageing population, there is also the fear that older people will use all the available resources. Younger people will be working simply to pay for the care of that generation of older people, and there will be nothing left to save for their own pensions.

Economic impact of age

Then there is research that shows we find it hard to place a value on those who no longer make an economic contribution. Although we can see children and young people as potential earners, and contributors, older people are simply sitting there waiting to die, unproductive, useless, economically inactive. Public policy reinforces that thinking, with most welfare reform policy work emphasising the need for people to get back into work, and regarding those who do not work as lazy, a drag on society and of little value.[18]

So the question of what old age is *for* becomes ever more pressing. If it merely reminds us of our mortality, of loss, of lack of value, of lack of productivity, of pointlessness, it is all too easy to see how prejudice against these parasites on society can grow. Even the limited praise of older people and association of various virtues with them, such as 'wisdom', 'experience', 'gravitas',[19] is usually associated with younger people *not* having those characteristics (for example, the

Conservative leader, David Cameron)[20] rather than with older people having them.

Yet this is completely different from other societies and cultures, where older people, even if there are large numbers of them, are valued very positively. The classic examples are China and Japan,[21] but the US also has a far more positive attitude to its elders than we do, and the political power of older people is a major factor in election campaigns.

Ageing is 'bad'

The real problem, however is that 'ageing', which should simply be a factual neutral term, is anything but. It has negative overtones however it is used, and we do not have either a positive attitude to ageing on the whole or a way of understanding ageing as a positive process in itself. Scientific advance tells us we can almost live forever, yet the cosmetic industry tells us all the time that we need to look younger. Facelifts, stomach tucks, neck lifts, Botox injections – they are all there to make us change ourselves into younger versions of ourselves. They are all there, and marketed powerfully, to make it clear that the image of the older person is distasteful or disgusting, and that it is in our power to make ourselves look younger than our calendar years, for the true depiction of old age is something to be avoided at all costs.[22]

Indeed, the Dove soap campaign at the end of 2005 seemed completely counter-intuitive, challenging our ageist attitudes and showing a model in her 90s advertising the soap as younger women were doing. There was a serious point being made in these advertisements – that we should love and accept our bodies (and wash them with Dove soap) whether young or old, fat or thin. But for many people the image itself was deeply shocking, and the acceptance of old age in all its glory and displaying it in the flesh clearly disturbed a considerable proportion of the public.

We would not normally celebrate a 90-year-old's body. Usually, we celebrate those who defeat their calendar age, whose looks belie their years,[23] and while we castigate the broadcasters for getting rid of newscasters in their 50s and early 60s, as happened to Moira Stuart at the BBC[24] – or for denying employment on age grounds, as happened to Selena Scott[25] – we also rejoice in looking at younger, more 'acceptable' faces on TV. Dames Helen Mirren and Judi Dench are celebrated because they do not look their age, while Joan Bakewell has written thoughtfully about how she misses being admired by men:

> While old men are thought to be ruggedly attractive, old women are deemed to be beyond allure, devoid of sexual chemistry, a worn husk of their juicier former selves. I remain true to my inner self: I still enjoy clothes, I still love high heels, have my hair tinted, watch my weight. I confront the mirror less often than I did, and when I do I make a harsh appraisal, and do my best with what's left.[26]

Yet Joan Bakewell is still working, as are Helen Mirren and Judi Dench, and the 97-year-old model for Dove Soap, Irene Sinclair – that may be partly why they get a different press, still having the power to move the public, and to attract, even if they are by any normal description 'old'. There is, however, an ironic addendum to Irene Sinclair's experience. When she was being visited by the talent scout for the Dove campaign, the 'casting director came round, but when I answered the door she pushed past me and said, "Is your mother here?". She didn't believe I could be 96.'

Challenging the champions

The by and large negative attitudes to older people are not helped, strangely, by the very organisations established to lobby in their interests. The 'age movement' itself contributes to the problem in some ways, and the increasing emphasis on dementia in the public mind – largely campaigned about, rightly, by Help the Aged and Age Concern, as well as by specialist charities such as the Alzheimer's Society – simply exacerbates the negative image of older people 'losing their marbles', not being able to cope.[27] Add to that the more traditional images used for fundraising of older people looking sad and lonely, or bent over and apparently very poor, collecting firewood, and the very organisations that are there to get rid of negative stereotypes of older people seem all too often to be using them.

Why it matters

So why should this matter? It is clear that more or less everyone is afraid of becoming old – including many older people. Indeed, once older people themselves have experienced some loss, either of loved ones or of faculties such as hearing or vision, they interpret this as the beginning of the end. Indeed, all too often they enter a spiral of depression and decline, and as this continues they do not expect to get better. It is, in their view, a one-way street.[28]

And this is despite evidence that many of these conditions, be it sight (cataract operations), hearing (digital hearing aids), arthritis (hip replacements), and depression itself (antidepressants and psychotherapeutic interventions), are clearly treatable. The facts do not match up to the assumptions, and the general assumption, by old and young alike, is that once the loss starts, there is no going back. This is reinforced by a whole range of images of older people in wider society, be it the hairdressers advertising a (cheaper) 'pensioner's hairdo'[29] or the beauty correspondents in newspapers telling older women thinking of a nip or a tuck, or simply very expensive face creams, that 'you are above all that now'.[30]

Becoming 'old'

There is a real improvement in the amount of attention being given to older people in newspapers and magazines, with advice for older women in *The Times*, such as that cited above, or *Vogue*'s annual issue focusing on older women, but it is not enough to counter the negative images of older people who will lose their sight or hearing or the capacity to walk or to drive. Once that loss of capability starts, you become – to your family, to yourself and to wider society – an 'old lady' with all the presumptions that go with that. You lose the force of your personality, in other people's minds and often in your own. You shrink back, and are diminished. Your place in society will have shifted to that of a user of services designed especially for you, but not in any way good enough, or imaginative enough, to make it possible for you to live your life as it was before.

Multiplying disadvantage

Those who are already disadvantaged by poor health and low income suffer disproportionately from these stereotypes, being seen as 'past it' earlier in their lives, and having a lower life expectancy as the gap in life expectancy between rich and poor has widened over the past 20 years or so. All older people get a free bus pass, but some have comments made to them by bus drivers that beggar belief, suggesting that some bus drivers see older people as a nuisance and as freeloaders, without realising that all they are doing is pushing older people back into their homes because they cannot cope with the speed at which they are expected to get on to the bus and find a seat.[31]

For those less well off, particularly, such services as are available and how they are provided and charged for tend to limit considerably older people's options in life. If Dial-a-ride services are used only by older people, they are often insufficiently generous and do not take people far enough, or to where they want to go. If day centres for older people are declining, as they are, the replacements that offer cross-generational interaction are few and far between, although often wonderful if they do exist. But the fact that most older people do not need or indeed want services targeted purely at and for them suggests we have done something very strange by treating older people as 'other' and different and not like us.

Manufacturing dependency

Peter Townsend has argued that the dependence of older people (in the 20th century) has been manufactured socially.[32] If you put older people in a separate basket and see them as frail and needy and poor and cold and not able to make decisions for themselves, requiring social workers to carry out needs assessments for them, you create a culture of dependency that is simply unnecessary. Given our ageing population, it does not make sense to see older people as any different from the rest of us – they are no needier, unless they are very frail. They can work – if they are allowed to – and they can certainly contribute to society. In almost all ways, they can do the same things, possibly more slowly or differently, as the rest of the population. If we stopped seeing them as old and just saw them as people, and listened to what they had to say about the services provided by local authorities and elsewhere, we would have a happier, and more productive, older population.

What do we do about this?

There is no doubt that older people need to fight the prejudice which holds them back, alongside younger people who are disturbed by what they see. There is virtually no empowerment narrative for ageing. Unlike other 'oppressed' groups, older people have not stood up proudly and declared their difference, demanding equal treatment despite differences. That is in part because older people do not see themselves – and, indeed, why should they? – as a single unit or class. They are whoever they were before, just older. Yet women drew attention to inequalities and fought for change, and they were as diverse as older people except in terms of gender – there is undoubtedly a need to do the same for older people. We need to see some angry older men and women, and although there are indeed some, there are not enough coming forward.

Age demands action

Yet there are some shining role models, such as the famous retired teacher, Rose Cottle, who, aged 102, demonstrated at number 10 Downing Street about the proposed closure of the care home she had lived in for 15 years, the Borehamwood Care Village in Hertfordshire; or Ken Mack, at 65 the lead campaigner against the closure of two care homes in Wrexham; or Melanie Phillips, who took up the cudgels to fight care home closures and evictions after Winifred Humphrey, also 102, had died 16 days after being evicted from the care home she had lived in for nine years to make room for a fee paying resident.[33]

Or there are those older people who campaign on the issue of post office services.[34] Or there is Josephine Rooney, who refused to pay her council tax because of the state of her street, dubbed 'crack alley' by the locals, and was jailed at age 69 for three months.[35] And there are growing signs of anger among older people in various local authorities around the country. But it is not enough.

So the questions remain. Can this group, if it is truly a group at all, achieve equality while denying the one characteristic that unifies them – old age? The answer is probably not. We need a grey power movement in the UK, and we need the voices of anger that we hear, clearly, but all too rarely, to articulate the injustices and the lack of respect that they come up against. We need more than a Dignity Champion in Sir Michael Parkinson, and a Voice of Older People in Dame Joan Bakewell, wonderful though what both of these two people do for older people is. It needs to be more political, and simply angrier.

Local authorities ought to be forced to consult older people about all planning applications that might affect them, and other decisions that are relevant, and older people should be able to say when public space does not suit them. The health services need to examine themselves – and there needs to be a vast programme of retraining of health professionals to sensitise them to issues of old age, and to make them realise that treating older people in an undignified fashion is not only cruel and unethical, but also simply poor-quality healthcare.

But these things will only happen if people get angrier. We have seen newspapers, especially *The Observer* and the *Daily Mail*, change and campaign for better treatment for older people on the wards of our hospitals. We have seen *The Times* in particular promote an award for achievement by older people (*The Times* Sternberg Active Life award, which started in 2008 and was won by Helen Bamber, founder of the Medical Foundation for the Victims of Torture). We have seen advertising move slightly to take account of the spending power of older people. But that is not enough, nor is it angry enough. We need to see more. And unless we do, using an empowerment and self-empowerment model to change things, we will not create a society that is comfortable with old age.

Age counts

That is only possible if we also challenge the assumption that older people are not valuable to society as a whole. It is clear that older people are seen by some people – and certainly by some institutions – as useless, as users of services rather than contributors. We should not be afraid to say that older people should contribute in some way as long as they can, whether in paid employment or as volunteers, whether by keeping an eye out for their neighbourhoods or by reading to children in schools. Older people are not victims and they are not pointless. They have much to do, much to learn and much to give. Nor should they automatically be given things cheaper because they are old, unless they are also poor, and they should not be left to live in poverty either, as many are. But to get these changes to come about, to be recognised as important and sensible and indeed essential, we need older people out there on the barricades, with a certain amount of rage in their hearts and fire in their bellies.

To the barricades

It is only Raymond Tallis, former Professor of Geriatric Medicine, who really mounts a call to the barricades as such. Even then he argues it for political reasons to do with liberty, more than for a change in the perception of older people themselves, although it would surely help if older people followed Tallis's lead. He argues that it is to older people themselves that we should be looking for criticism of the *status quo* on civil liberties and freedoms:

> Where, then, are we to look for the guardians of freedom? This is where the growing cadre of healthy elderly people may be increasingly important. They no longer yearn for promotion or preferment. They aren't required to bite their tongue or grovel. They have no targets to deliver on, no need to devote themselves to the futile productivity of academe, no asinine mission statements to write or respond to. They are at liberty to think and say what they like. They can therefore shout out what those who have families to feed or careers

to promote – and so must remain on message at all costs – would not dare mutter in their sleep. Because they have nothing to lose by speaking the truth….They are … a precious resource that we can ill afford to overlook….This is not an argument for a cognitive gerontocracy but a call for this new and growing generation of rentiers to take up the battle to defend the freedoms they have enjoyed but which, if present trends are unopposed, their grandchildren may not.[36]

Punch harder

So older people need to be out there campaigning, on a whole raft of issues, including those that are about old age itself. They need to campaign about compulsory retirement and take governments to task for falling in with the views of the Confederation of British Industry (CBI) and employers, that it is easier to have a retirement age than to do proper appraisals of every employee each year and get those no longer up to the mark to leave earlier and those who are still providing a good service to stay on. We need to challenge the link between old age and working age in general, as though they are by their very nature different. We need to describe ageing as it is, as a natural process, and to stop highlighting the exceptional and the 'national treasures' and instead tell it as it is, but encourage older people to take care of themselves and the health services to stop behaving in a discriminatory fashion.

And we need to get the anger and the spirit and the sheer strength of purpose of older people up in the headlines for the whole world to see – a real grey power movement, supported by age charities that stop thinking about victimhood and instead say that it is all there for us to change, if we were really serious about taking these issues on with older people, rather than on their unconsulted behalf.

Five things we can do now

1. There is space for a truly angry older age group.
2. The government should ensure that the Equality Bill lays the legislative building blocks for age equality, with a categorical ban on all forms of age discrimination.
3. Public services should be age-responsive and age-proof their provision.
4. End the default retirement age, and ensure everyone can carry on contributing for as long as they want.
5. Any organisation for older people should ensure zero tolerance for stereotyping and for patronising those it serves.

Notes

[1] Help the Aged (2002) *Marketing and advertising to older people*, London: Help the Aged.

[2] Media analysis report by Metrica for Help the Aged, 2004.

[3] Age Concern (2005) *How ageist is Britain?*, London: Age Concern.

[4] Ray, S., Sharp, E. and Abrams, D. (2006) *Ageism: A benchmark of public attitudes in Britain*, October, London: Age Concern England, p 7: 'Direct measures of people's experiences of unfair treatment on the basis of age, gender, race, religion, sexual orientation and disability showed that ageism was the most commonly experienced form of discrimination. Some 28% of respondents reported having experienced ageism in the past year'; p 50: 'The most serious form of discrimination was race or ethnicity (64% thought this was very or quite serious), followed by disability (54%) and then religion (51%). By comparison only 42% felt that ageism was very or quite serious and 52% felt that it was not very or not at all serious. Age was similar to gender and sexual orientation in that the prevailing view of the sample was that it was not serious as an equality issue.…The findings suggest that people feel benevolent prejudice is in general less serious than hostile prejudice. Old people, ie those aged 65–74 and in particular those of 75+, were less likely to view ageism as serious than the rest of the population.'

[5] Athill, D. (2008) *Somewhere towards the end*, London: Granta.

[6] Riddell, M. (2006) 'Longer lifespans are a bit of a grey area', *The Observer*, 12 February.

[7] Harries, C., Forrest, D., Harvey, N., McLelland, A. and Bowling, A. (2007) 'Which doctors are influenced by a patient's age? A multi-method study of angina treatment in general practice, cardiology and gerontology', *Quality and Safer Health Care*, vol 16, pp 23–7, doi: 10.1136/qshc.2006.018036; Help the Aged (2007) *Too old: Older people's accounts of discrimination, exclusion and rejection*, London: Help the Aged; Morris, J., Beaumont, D. and Oliver, D. (2006) 'Decent health care for older people', *BMJ*, vol 332, pp 1166–8 (20 May), doi: 10.1136/bmj.38835.669850.47 (published 5 May 2006).

[8] Bowling, A. and Dieppe, P. (2005) 'What is successful ageing and who should define it?', *BMJ*, vol 3312, pp 1548–51, 24 December.

[9] Ray, S., Sharp, E. and Abrams, D. (2006) *Ageism: A benchmark of public attitudes in Britain*, October, London: Age Concern England, p 7: 'Ageism takes the form of "benevolent prejudice" whereby older people are stereotyped as friendly, moral and admirable but less capable and less intelligent.… Older people are seen as warm but incompetent, ie "doddery but dear".'

[10] Bytheway, B., Ward, R., Holland, C. and Peace, S. (2007) *Too old: Older people's accounts of discrimination, exclusion and rejection*, A report from the Research on Age Discrimination Project (RoAD) to Help the Aged, p 31: '45% agree that films and advertisements portray older people as figures of fun.'

[11] Robinson, T., Callister, M., Magoffin, D. and Moore, J. (2007) 'The portrayal of older characters in Disney animated films', *Journal of Aging Studies*, vol 21, issue 3, August, pp 203–13.

[12] Cartoon: 'John Sergeant school of dance', *The Times*, 17 November 2008; Dunn, C. (2008) 'Dancing with the stars: like *Strictly* with extra pain', *The Guardian* 27 November (www.guardian.co.uk/culture/tvandradioblog/2008/nov/27/dancing-with-the-stars).

[13] Cartoons focusing on Menzies Campbell's age from 20 and 22 September 2006, 15 September 2007, 15 October 2007 (www.timesonline.co.uk/tol/template/2.0-0/element/pictureGalleryPopup.jsp?id=2666341&&offset=0&&sectionName=Politics).

[14] Elderspeak and the effect on older people's health: Leland, J. (2008) 'In "sweetie" and "dear", a hurt for the elderly', *New York Times*, 7 October (www.nytimes.com/2008/10/07/us/07aging.html?-r=1&scp=1&sq=Elderspeak&st=nyt).

[15] Ray, S., Sharp, E. and Abrams, D. (2006) *Ageism: A benchmark of public attitudes in Britain*, October, London: Age Concern England, p 42: 'the overall numbers are high and this may include some people who thought of family members as friends'; ibid, p 8: 'policies which segregate older people (eg within healthcare, social care or housing) need to be considered carefully in light of their potential effects on ageism within society.'

[16] Street-Porter, J. (2005) 'Our ageist attitudes have got to change', *Independent*, 8 September.

[17] Ray, S., Sharp, E. and Abrams, D. (2006) *Ageism: A benchmark of public attitudes in Britain*, October, London: Age Concern England, p 63.

[18] Help the Aged (2007) *Consultation response – Discrimination Law Review, a framework for fairness: Proposals for a single Equality Bill for Great Britain*, September, p 97: economic contributions: 'people over the age of 60 contribute 792 million voluntary hours per year; it is estimated that people over 60 years contribute up to £50 billion each year in unpaid family care;... those aged 50 years and over are major consumers,... accounting for 45% of the total consumer spend'; also: Kingston, P. (2008) 'Education potential of older people "untapped"', *The Guardian*, 22 October: 'The mental capital of older people is a massive and under-utilised resource' (www.guardian.co.uk/education/2008/oct/22/mental-capital-older-people).

[19] Zuckerman, A. (2008) 'Wisdom from famous over 65s', *The Times*, 27 September (http://women.timesonline.co.uk/tol/life_and_style/women/the_way_we_live/article4802662.ece).

[20] Wintour, P. (2008) 'I am a man with a Thatcherite reform plan, says Cameron', *The Guardian*, 2 October: Cameron's conference speech in which he said that the worth of leadership lay not in experience, but in judgement, values

and character (www.guardian.co.uk/politics/2008/oct/02/davidcameron.
toryconference).

[21] Japan has a 'Respect the Aged' Day, but also negative comments: Lewis, L. (2008) 'Japanese Prime Minister Taro Aso condemns "hobbling malingerers"', *The Times*, 28 November (www.timesonline.co.uk/tol/news/world/asia/article5248197.ece).

[22] There is widespread use of anti-ageing beauty products; for example, L'Oréal offers anti-wrinkle, anti-brown spot and anti-ageing products; recent scientific study on antioxidants as an antidote to ageing: Randerson, J. (2008) 'Blow to vitamins as antidote to ageing', *The Guardian*, 1 December (www.guardian.co.uk/science/2008/dec/01/medical-research-health-vitamin-supplements).

[23] Celebrities growing old gracefully: 'Susan Sarandon has still got that certain something at 61', *The Guardian*, 30 July 2008 (www.guardian.co.uk/lifeandstyle/gallery/2008/jul/30/celebrity?picture=336061778); *Hello Magazine*, 'Diana Ross rolls back the years at Nobel gig', 12 December 2008 (www.hellomagazine.com/celebrities-news-in-pics/12-12-2008/50364/).

[24] Martin, N. (2007) 'Moira Stuart quits, reigniting BBC ageism row', *Telegraph*, 4 October (www.telegraph.co.uk/news/uknews/1564966/Moira-Stuart-quits,-reigniting-BBC-ageism-row.html);(www.guardian.co.uk/lifeandstyle/gallery/2008/jul/30/celebrity?picture=336057352).

[25] Scott, S. (2009) 'No, I'm *not* too old', *Daily Mail*, 11 April.

[26] Bakewell, J. (2006) 'What I see in the mirror', *The Guardian*, 7 October.

[27] Bond, J., Peace, S., Dittmann-Kohli, F. and Westerhof, G. (eds) (2007) *Ageing in Society*, London: Sage Publications; for example, p 305: 'being demented remains one of the most negative stereotypes of old age and one that is increasingly in the public eye because of increasing prevalence in the community and the role of advocate organisations to raise awareness.'

[28] Ibid, p 304: 'A common feature of constructions of ageing and old age is the inevitable decline in physical appearance and fitness, and cognitive performance. The emphasis on decline rather than change underpins the almost universal negative stereotypes and attitudes of ageing and older people that appear to be held by most people of all ages and cultures.'

[29] Bytheway, B., Ward, R., Holland, C. and Peace, S. (2007) *Too old: Older people's accounts of discrimination, exclusion and rejection*, A report from the Research on Age Discrimination Project (RoAD) to Help the Aged, p 36: 'the marketing strategies employed by the hairdressing and fashion industries help to perpetuate ideas about what kind of "look" is appropriate (and inappropriate) for both older and younger people [eg 'pensioner's hairdo', p 32]. This in turn affects people's ability to express themselves freely through their appearance as they age.'

[30] Vine, S. (*Times* beauty editor) (2008) 'Defy your age', *The Times*, 7 January; tips to defy your age for over-65s: 'If you succumbed to breast implants in your younger years, now might be a good time to have them taken out, as a young woman's bosoms on an older frame is not a good look. Besides, you are above all that now. Instead, cultivate an aura of grandeur' (http://women. timesonline.co.uk/tol/life_and_style/women/beauty/article3141009.ece).

[31] Help the Aged (2007) *Less equal than others: Public responses to government proposals on age discrimination*, London: Help the Aged, p 7f, p 8: 'I should like to see Jeremy Paxman cope without losing his temper if he was shouted at to "get on the bus – you've got two seconds".'

[32] Townsend, P. (1981) 'The structured dependency of the elderly: a creation of social policy in the twentieth century', *Ageing & Society*, vol 1, pp 5–28; p 5: 'the dependency of the elderly in the twentieth century is being manufactured socially and its severity is unnecessary.'

[33] Phillips, M. (2003) 'And we call this a welfare state?', *Daily Mail*, 9 July.

[34] North Staffordshire Pensioners' Convention, BBC News, 19 July 2007.

[35] *Daily Telegraph*, 27 June 2006.

[36] Tallis, R. (2006) 'To the barricades, old codgers: you're the last bastions of threatened liberty', *The Times*, 31 July.

SIX

A life worth living?
Quality of life in older age

Bryan Appleyard

- Seventeen per cent of older people have less than weekly contact with family, friends and neighbours, and 11 per cent have less than monthly contact.[1]
- Seven out of 10 older people have never used the internet.[2]
- Seventy per cent of 25- to 44-year-olds have recently attended an arts event, compared with just over 40 per cent of the over-75s.

Boomers beating biology

'After 60 – no matter what – your skin can let you down,' says Jane Fonda in a 2009 television advertisement for a L'Oréal skincare product for older women.

It seems like only yesterday – it was, in fact, 1982 – that Fonda, then 45, was teaching us to tone our bodies in her first *Workout* video. In doing so, she launched the exercise craze of the 1980s with all the attendant glorifications of the perfect, gym-fit body. It was an aspect of the age's yearning for self actualisation, the belief in the autonomous, monadic self that also produced the financial imperative 'greed is good' and, in a weak moment, Margaret Thatcher's remark that there is 'no such thing as society'.

'The human body', said Wittgenstein, 'is the best picture of the human soul.' The soul of the 1980s was lean, greedy, super-fit and far too young for its years. But then again, as Fonda tells us, after 60 your skin can let you down – no matter what. Yet, even after 60, we must remain fervent self-actualisers – what else is there to do? Being young is the only game in town. We must act to halt the decline of our skin tone because, as L'Oréal advertisements always insist, 'We're worth it'.

Having it all

Fonda, although born in 1937, is a baby boomer heroine. The generation born between 1945 and 1964 forms a thickish cohort that, from the 1980s onwards, grew edgy about their ageing bodies. This was, after all, the generation that had everything – liberation, in the 1960s, from the oppressive sexual mores of the past, unprecedented increases in affluence, the glittering gadgets of a technological explosion – and, as a result, was unused to being denied anything. And yet here, in the mirror, was slackening skin, a sure sign that they could not have eternal youth, that death stalked their Arcadia.

The irony was that having, in their minds, repudiated the lives of their parents, the boomers now found their bodies were betraying them, turning them into replicas of their mothers and fathers whether they liked it or not. But here was Fonda, star of *Barbarella*, old enough to be their mother, just, *and* with a perfect body. It could be done. It must be done.

Fighting the signs

This pressure to 'fight the signs of ageing', as another ad puts it, is now applied at every turn. You cannot leave the house – or stay in the house with a newspaper or with the TV on – without being told to do something about your failing flesh. I was thinking of this sitting in a hairdresser's (there are very few barbers left, something one notices at 57) staring at a range of products called Dermologica AGE Smart. Afterwards, on the internet I learn that the £37.50 AGE Smart starter kit 'contains a full month's regimen you can use every day for firmer, smoother, healthier skin'. ('Can' use every day? Surely they mean 'must'?) In *Elle* magazine Annet King of Dermalogica's own Dermal Institute explains:

> There is nothing you can apply to your skin that can make you look ten years younger and nothing can eliminate wrinkles, so instead you have to be smart about preventing the biochemical reactions that make skin age.

So, Annet, we must affect a mature acceptance of the depredations of age, but, at the same time and at any cost, resist.

Meanwhile, the *Daily Mail* tells me that the actress Julia Roberts is 'fabulous at 41' and that Britney Spears is 'back in shape' with a 'finely toned tummy'. It was only a year ago that the *Mail* was reporting on Britney's 'unsightly elephant legs'. Has she still got them? Is the tummy a one-off improvement? It hardly matters. She will sag in the end and, doubtless, soon enough, Julia's fall from fabulousness will be chronicled in savage detail.

Another autobiographical moment: some years ago, I was on *Newsnight* on BBC2 discussing Bob Dylan's artistic self-reinvention in 1997 when he was 56. 'Isn't it a bit absurd', asked the presenter (I am quoting from memory), 'for a rock star to be carrying on at that age?'

'You mean', I replied, 'like stupid old Titian or boring old Rembrandt still banging away with their self-portraits?' I also meant to quote Yeats – 'Why should not old men be mad?' – but the moment was past. Note the assumption. Rock is art – it has to be, boomers made it – but it is unique among arts in that it is only for the young.

Paying for age

For some time the World Bank, among others, has been gloomy about the 'demographic time-bomb'. Thanks to higher life expectancies and lower birth rates among baby boomers, the average age in the developed world is rising. Over the next 25 years, for example, the number of people aged 80 and over in the European Union will treble. And they will all be high-maintenance boomers.

'In the language of demography', writes Alan Walker, Professor of Social Policy at the University of Sheffield, 'the population pyramid is bulging and fast becoming cone-shaped.' Fewer young people will be supporting more old ones. The young will not like it – they will want to inherit the world and get on with it but they won't be able to because of all these oldies blocking their path. Pressure groups have been formed.

'Because of the labour market in Germany,' I was told by Dr Jorg Tremmel for the Foundation for the Rights of Future Generations, 'the present young are known as Generation Internship because they can't get paid jobs. In 1970 a 30-year-old was earning 15 per cent less than a 50-year-old. Now the gap is 40 per cent.'

Impulsion Concorde, another such group in France, has the slogan 'We will not pay your debt.' And in Israel there is the Commission for Future Generations, designed to ensure that the current older generation does not impoverish its successors. The boomers, once the protestors, are now the protestees.

'How can the old seize everything?' Avner Offer, Professor of Economic History at Oxford, once said to me. 'The young will rebel.... They'll simply go on strike.'

Stop being old or we won't work – that's some platform. A tricky one too, since older people are not even allowed to die. I learn from the *Japan Times* that an ageing population is leading to a crematoria crisis

– there are not enough to cope with the 1.1 million people who die annually in Japan. Japan has the longest life expectancy in the world – over 78 for men and over 85 for women. The Nippon Foundation has one answer: floating crematoria, incinerations at sea 'bypassing the "not-in-my-backyard syndrome" and saving on real estate'. Not even by dying can older people stop being a burden on society.

The youth imperative

We get the message. The world wants longevity but it does not want old age. Dying is bad, to be avoided at all costs, but so is decrepitude. Being old is unthinkable. Contemporary pop culture is predicated on this idea: how *dare* Bob Dylan still get up on stage and sing some of the most beautiful songs ever written *as if he were still a young man?* Such a question could only be asked in a climate of philistine youth worship.

Reinforcing this, the tabloids and the celebrity magazines feast gleefully on young bodies and then gloat when they show signs of decline. (I say 'tabloids', but the term is intended to include the increasingly tabloid sections of broadsheets and previously austere TV news shows. Nobody now resists the youth and celebrity cult. Their marketing departments would not let them.) It may look as though they are having their cake and eating it – one body providing a story on the way up and then another on the way down – and, indeed, they are, but there is more to it than that.

You do not have to be a psychiatrist to detect the underlying sublimation of terror and disgust. The fading body is derided, mocked, in an attempt to distance the unacceptable truth of ageing. And why does this happen so much now? Because, thanks to the demographics and healthcare, the perfect, unfaded body is everywhere. In response, advertisements and editorials paint the world in the colours of soft porn – images that say you *can* be like this, therefore, you *should* be like this. And, if you are not, you will get torn apart in the press.

Occasionally, the tabloids will balance the cultish adoration of youth with stories like that of Julia Roberts's 41-year-old fabulousness. But of course, such stories make matters worse because what they are really saying is she does not look 41, she looks much younger. She is right to do so, she is *virtuous* to do so, this is an achievement. It takes effort, time, exercise, diet and, probably, yoga or Pilates. She must be doing something right, she cannot be allowed to be just lucky because, if it were just her genes, that would subvert the rationale of the same newspaper's health and fitness pages. Why bother buying this stuff if your bodily destiny is fixed at birth? Gorgeous Julia must put the hours in and the money out. For women beyond a certain age *not* to fling themselves into some intensive regime of youth preservation is a crime against the prevailing moral climate.

Perhaps, you might think, she has better things to do with her time: read a book or something. Don't be absurd, this is *the best thing* to do. It is not, as L'Oréal claims, that 'you're worth it'; rather it is that you won't be worth anything at all if you don't do it. It's not you that's worth it, it's this pot of largely ineffective but reassuringly expensive cream. Or, for the wealthy and, increasingly, the not so wealthy, there is cosmetic surgery. Ads in the tube, on TV, in the press offer youth at the end of a scalpel, a liposuction tube or a syringe full of Botox. We're worth it.

Let me also tease out the subtext of the only slightly more respectable horror stories of the demographic time-bomb, of economic, fiscal and political meltdown caused by the bloated cohort of the tired, idle old suffocating the dreams of the energetic, hard-working young. Along with global warming, this must rate as one of the great unintended consequences of our time. Medicine and public health measures keep people alive – that is what they are for. Vaccination, antibiotics, effective sewerage and the suppression of infant mortality were all unarguable goods that massively extended life expectancy in the 20th century. But, combined with the unfortunate but well-known fact that the modern rich tend to have fewer babies, they will inevitably cause the population to age uncontrollably. Is that a problem? Apparently. The implication of these stories is that from these many goods, the one big bad of hordes of old people follows.

The threat of longevity

But why must an ageing population be a bad thing? Isn't that exactly what we wanted? I seem to remember John Mortimer once saying that no vice was worth giving up for an extra two years in a nursing home. But if we do give up and keep out of the nursing home, alive and fit, what is wrong with that?

The assumptions behind the demographic time-bomb idea are obvious. First, older people – all of them, apparently – will be an economically negative force and, second, they will be egregiously selfish in their behaviour, hoarding assets and plundering the wealth of the working young.

'Everywhere', writes Professor Pat Thane of these time-bomb stories, 'this is presented gloomily. Old people are described as helpless dependants, imposing burdens of healthcare and pensions on a shrinking population of younger workers.'[3]

Age helps: the economic upside

Both the time-bomb assumptions are demonstrably false or, at the very least, overstated. Another effect of improved healthcare is the improved fitness of older people, who, as a result, can work longer. Indeed, a report from HSBC, *The future of retirement*, in 2007[4] found just this. Around the world 11 per cent of people in their 70s and a third of people in their 60s were working. Research by Goldman Sachs[5] demonstrates the boost to gross domestic product (GDP) that occurs with higher participation rates in older age such as these. Also, they do not seem to be that selfish. All the well-off grandparents I know are eager to share their wealth with their grandchildren. The assumptions are also disgracefully mechanistic because they imply that there is no counterbalancing value in the existence of large numbers of old people.

First and last, we seem to be being judged only as economic units. The idea that old people bring wisdom, experience, memory, continuity and the kinds of talents that can come only from years of work is entirely absent from this calculus. Like the cosmetics ads and the tabloid stories, the reporters of the 'demographic time-bomb' seem consumed by the conviction that oldness is always and everywhere a bad thing.

Elder statesmen

And then there are the politicians. Pat Thane points out that, not so long ago, old men – Brezhnev, Churchill, Eisenhower, de Gaulle, Adenauer – strutted the world stage. Not only were they old, they did not try to disguise the fact. Indeed, there was something comforting about the idea of the elder statesman. Even their acts were reported by old men. The Americans' most trusted TV 'anchor' was Walter Cronkite, who was anchoring away until he was 65 and whose most defining feature was his consoling, grandfatherly manner. In Britain we had similarly venerable figures such as Andrew Gardner, who was not actually old but looked and acted as if he was.

But by the end of the century, Pat Thane observes, 'most states had younger leaders, elected in their 40s or 50s'. And, of course, they try to look even younger. Nothing more characterised the Blair–Clinton years than the exaggerated bounciness with which our leaders leapt to the podium. It was spin, of course, a sure sign of youth cult marketing invading politics.

It was different, as the Americans say, 'back in the day'. In July 1966 I remember Harold Wilson – a man who appeared to have been born middle-aged with a pipe in his mouth – reopening The Cavern, the Liverpool club where The Beatles began their careers. The message was clear: a grandee was slumming it a little to tell the young it was OK to be young. For a while. Tony Blair, in contrast, had Noel Gallagher of Oasis round for drinks at Downing Street. The message was equally clear and utterly different: 'I am no grandee, I am young like you.' Gallagher was calling the shots, The Beatles were just serfs.

Youth defines age

My central point is that the quality of life of older people is primarily dependent on the attitudes of younger people. But, importantly, the reverse is also true because, as John Donne warned us, 'No man is an island, entire of itself.' The overarching and, for me, unarguable statement is that quality of life is dependent on others.

This suggests a definition of that elusive 'quality of life'. I am impressed by the profound discussions I have read about the meanings and metrics of life quality. I am impressed by the practical aspirations – they are attempts to improve real things in the real world. But this, it seems to me, is the surprisingly simple heart of the matter. Nothing has more impact on the quality of my life than the attitudes of those I come into contact with directly or indirectly via the media, advertising, marketing and the political and social climate in which I live.

Our selves are not the autonomous, monadic beings celebrated by the workouts and greed of the 1980s, by the dominant boomer ideology, nor are they 'worth it' in the sense intended by L'Oréal, and they are especially not the atoms of economic theory. Our selves are social entities, meaningless until defined by the lives of others, living and dead. We cannot thrive without identity, recognition, belonging and acceptance. Or, more exactly, there is nothing to thrive in such conditions. The quality of life is the quality of all life, not just mine. The best way to improve the quality of life of the young is to improve that of the old and, again, *vice versa*.

In these terms, it becomes clear why my subsidiary statement – that the quality of older life is dependent on younger attitudes – needs to be emphasised now. As my opening suggested, the young – and, indeed, the old – are being encouraged to turn against older people by a malign combination of pop culture, body fascism and political rhetoric. The young are being encouraged to believe that, from the age of about 14, life is an unremittingly downward slope involving increasingly desperate struggles to patch up one's fast-waning charms.

This view is unredeemed even by wit. Once Marilyn Monroe could sing (as recently as 1959), 'Get that ice or else no dice'. Look after yourself in old age, girls. It is an index of the progressive debauchery and infantilisation of popular culture that it is now inconceivable that a song such as 'Diamonds are a girl's best friend' could be regarded as having hit potential since it is predicated on the shameful, the unspeakable fact that 'we all lose our charms in the end'. No marketing man would countenance such a morbid, counter-cultural product. You can get wrecked on drugs, like Amy Winehouse, but not on years. Marilyn, sadly, did not live up to the wit of the song.

I suppose it is that 'we' in the song that is the problem as it draws attention to the fact that everybody grows old. Pop culture is perfectly at ease with the view that older people are charmless, but only on the condition that they are a 'you' or a 'they', not a 'we'. The arc of life from childhood to old age barely seems to exist in the popular imagination. Instead we see life in blocks. It is as if, somehow, older people are an entirely static cohort and young people are forever young. The idea is celebrated in the teen line about living fast, dying young and leaving a beautiful corpse. In his film *The Doors*, Oliver Stone, a supremely boomer director, makes this explicit. After Jim Morrison, The Doors' lead singer, dies, his body and features wrecked by 'living fast', we see his corpse. The face has been magically returned to his youthful beauty. What, exactly, is the message here? *Ars longa vita brevis*? Or that the beauty and youth are more true than the drug-induced premature ageing?

Acceptance of ageism

This blockish view of youth and age is reinforced by the marketing idea of 'segmentation', the division of the population into groups defined by various factors, the most common being age. Marketing people find good reasons for believing in a bad thing – the politics of identity. To be old is to be only old, just as to be black is to be only black. This may seem harmless but, ultimately, it leads to the unspoken suspicion that older people are not full participants in the show, that they are not fully human.

Actually, it's not that unspoken. The inhuman old feeling is, I think, why older people are the only group it is acceptable to abuse. TV sitcoms cannot make jokes based on the shortcomings of blacks, Jews, women or people with disabilities, but they are always making jokes about the failings of the older generation. 'Old people fart and don't know it' was one peculiarly nasty laugh line I recently heard on an American show. This is definitely laughing *at* older people, not with them. It is astounding that it can happen at all in a politically correct world so hyper-sensitive to the power of words to offend entire groups. But contemporary priggery does not seem to extend its dubious protection to older people.

Representation *versus* reality

Stepping back a little, it is important to be clear that what I am talking about here is representation. I do not believe most young people really think they will never get old. I do not think most economists do not value older people. I also see that fear and disgust have always been aspects of our response to old age. Old people – women especially – have often been seen as dangerous or frightening throughout history. There was never, as people often claim, some golden age when senior citizens were consistently venerated or at least respected. The spectacle of age has always been seen by some as a threat.

My point is not that anti-age attitudes are new, or even that they are consciously held to the point where people would express them as opinions. Rather, my point is that we are, today, possessed of an unprecedented power to exploit, disseminate and reinforce ideas, prejudices and myths. This power is deployed to promote a cult of youth and a dismissal of age. The young – 'hard bodies' in the significant slang of sexual predation – carry all the high cards. They alone must be wooed and pampered. As a result, any existing negative attitudes to older people are massively amplified to the point where they become a sort of universal backdrop, a steady body of presuppositions, to the entire culture.

A market – and a resource

Why this should have happened is, in part, a mystery. Francis Fukuyama, the American political economist, said to me some years ago that he was baffled that, in spite of the increasing numbers of over-50s and at £91 billion a year their considerable spending power, advertising and marketing were still overwhelmingly targeted at the young. The world is full of WOOPIES – well-off older persons – but the media do not seem to or would rather not notice. This remains true. I see TV ads for holidays, pensions, savings schemes and stairlifts for older people because they are rare, almost exotic, and not generally on prime time.

That time slot is overwhelmingly and illogically reserved for the luring of the lesser wealth of the young.

I cannot solve this mystery any more than Fukuyama could, but I do think the new, hyper-connected world is a part of the explanation. One of the many hot new terms in marketing is 'viral'. It comes from the internet and it refers to the way that, for example, a video on YouTube can go from having a few views to millions. It is said to have gone 'viral' because it mimics the reproductive energy of a virus. Good youth has gone viral, as has its opposite, bad age.

Reasons to be cheerful?

Yet it is here, I think, that I can begin to insert a note of optimism – or at least a sign that the youth cult of marketing may be missing the point. In August 2006 Peter Oakley, a 79-year-old pensioner from Leicester who had taken an IT course, launched himself on YouTube as Geriatric1927. He simply presented a kind of video diary of his thoughts and impressions. It was entirely gimmick-free and yet, within a week, Geriatric1927 had gone viral. It was the site's number one video. The last time I looked, this first episode had been viewed 2.8 million times. The viewers were young and they got in touch, writing him surprisingly intimate letters. I asked Oakley why he thought his videos had taken off among the young. 'There are so many people,' he said, 'who haven't spoken to their grandparents, or their grandparents are dead. They seem to see me as a grandparent with whom they can converse....They pour out their hearts to me.'

This, I believe, is not quite so much a case of clutching at straws as it may seem. Oakley's story may be anecdotal evidence, it may be a flash in the pan, but it is supported, I think, by most people's experience. There is a natural relationship between grandparents and grandchildren which is distinct and profound. In Oakley, his young correspondents found a surrogate grandfather who, like real ones, performed a role that could not be performed by parents, siblings or friends. One could define this role in terms of a certain distance combined with intense intimacy and concern. But precise definitions do not matter. The point is that it can only be fulfilled by a significantly older relative. Or, to put it more generally, there is something here, something immensely valuable, that only older people can do. This insight subverts the industrialised marketing of the youth cult by showing how much we are in danger of losing.

So, to summarise, there is a tension between ordinary, naturally occurring human concerns and feelings that would accord a distinct and vital place for older people and the prevailing, financially self-interested and, ultimately, cruel cultural norms that would dismiss the older generation as irrelevant or a nuisance.

Attitudes to dying

I can now take this one step further by saying this tension is heightened by the post-war boomer generation's lack of an emotional and imaginative grip on the arc of life from birth to death. Again I am generalising, but it is generalities that exert the most force in the broad cultural context.

The boomers' lack is best seen from the point of view of death. In 1965, in the midst of the boomers' golden age of youth culture, Geoffrey Gorer published a book entitled *Death, grief and mourning in contemporary Britain*. This was inspired by the response of his friends after the death of his brother. 'They clearly no longer had any guidance from ritual', he wrote, 'as to the way to treat a self-confessed mourner.'

Death embarrassed a people who had become used to a ritual of dying involving doctors, nurses, drugs and, above all, denial. As a result, Gorer wrote in an essay that anticipated his book, death had become as embarrassing and as subversively titillating as sex had been for the Victorians: 'There seem to be a number of parallels between the fantasies which titillate our curiosity about the mystery of sex, and those which titillate our curiosity about the mystery of death.'

The great historian Philippe Aries took up Gorer's theme at the end of his masterpiece *The hour of our death*. He contrasted the good 18th-century death – in full awareness and surrounded by friends and relatives – with the modern death. About the latter he particularly stresses the denials involved in contemporary death: 'And everyone becomes an accomplice to a lie born of this moment which later grows to such proportions that death is driven into secrecy. The dying person and those around him continue to play a comedy in which "nothing has changed", "life goes on as usual", and "anything is still possible".'

I believe there is a direct line to be drawn from these insights and the art of Damien Hirst, the most valuable contemporary artistic name in the world today. Hirst's work consists largely of *memento mori*, reminders of our mortality, of the most crude kind. His chopped-up animals are intended to show that we are, ultimately, no more than rotting flesh. His most famous work – the shark corpse floating in a tank of formaldehyde – is called *The physical impossibility of death in the mind of someone living*. Such works could only be made and bought for astronomical sums in a culture that finds ageing and death unacceptable, taboo. They titillate by breaking the taboo. And it is pretty clear that if you get your thrills from dwelling on the idea that we are 'nothing but' rotting flesh, then you are never going to be comfortable with the spectacle of old people.

Now, it may be said that this is easily explained as an aspect of secularism. A society without faith is inevitably going to have trouble with decline and death. But secularism has been around for a long time and the phenomenon defined by Gorer and Aries and underlined by Hirst is distinctly contemporary. There is also nothing necessarily secular about the reductivist, nothing-but ideology that underpins the nihilistic thrill of the sight of rotting flesh. Rather, a specialist subcategory of secularism is at work. This is the secularism of affluence, relative peace, mass media and rapid technological innovation: the secularism, in a word, of distraction from the facts of life. This is boomer secularism. Discomfort and denial when confronted with the hard fact of life's arc – the lies in the intensive care unit, the shark in the tank – are all aspects of the state of mind that sustains the cult of youth.

The unspoken calculus

All of this feeds into the unspoken calculus of life's value. If we do not have a humane sense of the span of human life, then we incline to the simple-minded view that young hours are more valuable than old. *In extremis* – saving a 10-year-old before an 80-year-old from a fire – one might indeed make such a judgement. But to apply these extreme judgements to everyday life is to create a world devoid of hope, a world in which one can only ever be in decline. That we are doing precisely this was brutally captured by the brilliant satirist Chris Morris in his spoof TV news show *The Day Today*. Reporting on a bomb in Oxford Street, he said five people had been killed but 'being old, they would have been dead soon anyway'. Morris is one of the most penetrating observers of what lies beneath Britain today. If he sees it, it is there.

The way out of all this is unclear. There are some (Fukuyama is one of them) who argue that the 'great disruption' of the 1960s, the boomers' favourite decade, will gradually unwind as moral impulses based more firmly on human nature re-assert themselves. If he is right, then the grandfather-need on which Peter Oakley stumbled is a straw in a very promising wind. A more rooted, humane view of old age will be restored and the media will be obliged to adjust as their previous attitudes become unacceptable.

I am doubtful, perhaps because I am so aware of the astonishing power of the media and their obsession with youth. They have, as reality TV shows demonstrate daily, a tyrannical ability to alter the minds and behaviour of their audiences. It is, to my mind, entirely natural to have a sufficiently strong sense of modesty and decorum to recoil from the very idea of such shows. Unfortunately, it is equally natural to succumb to an age's demands when couched in professionally seductive terms. The defence of the producers and marketing people is always 'it's what people want', but, of course, they create the people that want these things. How, for example, did we know we wanted to watch poor, cancer-stricken Jade Goody face the end of her life in public until she appeared on *Big Brother*, and then even learned of her diagnosis on another country's version of the same show?

For the moment, therefore, if, as I argue, the quality of life of older people is primarily dependent on the attitudes of the younger, there is a problem that will not, in the foreseeable future, go away. What, then, is to be done?

Reconnecting society

In terms of changing the culture, it is perfectly legitimate to mock, deride, scorn and complain about cheap anti-old gags and mindlessly youth-dominated media. Personally, I don't mind the cheap gags as long as older people are free to make similar jokes about everybody else. A free, post-discriminatory day will have dawned when everybody feels free to laugh at everybody else. And the youth-dominated media are, as Fukuyama effectively said, a bizarre case of market failure, caused by the youth-mania of our mediacrats. The more often this is pointed out, the sooner older people will have their share of the public realm.

But that is the supply side. There is also a demand side of this equation. Do older people want to participate in the culture or are they content to watch the young? The liberal-minded, knee-jerk answer to this is yes, they do want to be involved or, at least, they should. This is not, on closer examination, self-evident.

First, they would be right to reject efforts to involve them like the recent scheme in some cinemas – OAP screenings of movies that included tea and biscuits. So we could have gay screenings with light beers and Metropolitan cocktails, screenings for women with pinafores and knitting needles, and Caribbean screenings with ganja and goat curry? I thought not.

Second, they may not wish to participate in this particular culture because, as I have said, it is designed to exclude them. They may be happier in their own alternative culture.

Third – this is another version of the same point, although there is plenty of evidence that older people are like everybody else – they thrive on social contact. I do not think the evidence suggests that they or anybody else thrive in a mass, hyper-connected media culture. In other words, we should be sensitive to the possibility that it may not be good for anybody simply to adapt what we have now to accommodate older people – building, as it were, virtual access ramps in cyberspace.

More time to have a life ... but less time spent having one

That said, the evidence is that old people are being unnecessarily excluded for no good reason (I am using figures provided by Help the Aged). Perhaps the most dramatic example of this comes from museum and gallery visits, something that might be expected to be precisely the sort of activity one might reserve for one's later years. In fact, only 25 per cent of over-75s had been to either a museum or a gallery in the previous 12 months compared to 40 per cent for 65- to 74-year-olds and 46 per cent for 24- to 64-year-olds. There may be mobility and access issues involved, although the fact that 32 per cent of people with a limiting disability responded positively suggests that there is a specific age factor.

Similar figures emerge for other activities. Only 38 per cent of over-75s are involved in the arts compared with 59 per cent of 16- to 24-year-olds, 45 per cent have attended an arts performance compared with 66 per cent, 45 per cent have access to multi-channel TV compared with 78 per cent, and, most starkly, only 22 per cent of over-75s take part in sport compared with 89 per cent of 16- to 24-year-olds. Only five per cent of over-75s are involved in learning and nine per cent of 65- to 74-year-olds.

The glib response to such figures is 'Well, what do you expect? They are old'. But this is, of course, to indulge the unspoken calculus, the view that old hours are intrinsically less worthwhile than young ones. All of these activities are precisely what older people should be doing in large numbers. They involve, inspire and stimulate (so does reading a decent book, but that seems to be looking after itself: library usage shows little variation by age).

The question is: why aren't they doing these things? Physical inability may be part of the problem – but only part, as people with

Figure 6.1: Participation in activities, by age

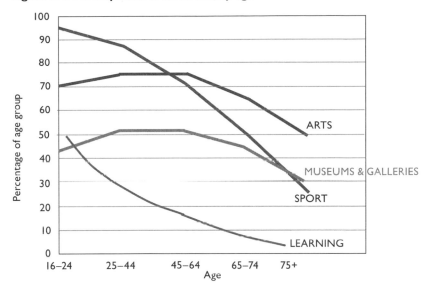

Based on Department of Culture, Media and Sport, 'Taking Part' survey (2007)

disabilities generally participate more than older people. In addition, as I have said, older people are much fitter than they used to be. In some areas – perhaps multi-channel TV or activities not covered by these figures, such as surfing the net or listening to downloaded music – technophobia may play a part. But, however you frame the issue, you are left with the irreducible and not convincingly explained fact of elderly non-participation.

I am sceptical of any remedy that remotely resembles the tea-and-biscuit film screenings for OAPs. Of course, steps should be taken to ensure that any obstacles to the participation of older people are removed. But they should not be taken condescendingly because this inevitably entrenches the prejudice that older people are different, that they are not quite 'one of us' and that prejudice is entrenched in the minds of older people as much as in the minds of the young. Discrimination in every form has the effect of convincing discriminatees that they are, indeed, different.

Unfortunately, condescension is the nearest thing to an acceptable attitude towards older people to be found among the youth-crazed. The block view of demography – 'the old are not us and we are forever young' – encourages a range of attitudes that runs only from condescension to contempt or ignorance. (Again, I stress that this is not a universal condemnation of everybody under 50. I am simply saying that a negative view of older people is implicit in the disproportionate celebration of the young and, as a result, will be manifested, often unconsciously, throughout our culture.) In this context, specific anti-exclusion devices may help, but they will not address the underlying problem.

Just people like us

The best hope, I believe, is threefold. First, the demographic reality of a much older population will finally sink into the minds of the media, marketing and advertising executives who are the only people with the power to truly remodel the environment in which attitudes are formed. There is reason for hope here. Those businesses are still dominated by baby boomers – roughly people aged 50 to 65 – and they now have a real interest in moving on from the celebration of youth culture, a phenomenon for which they were responsible in the first place.

Second, the presence of more, fitter old people may repair some of the damage done by the replacement of the extended by the nuclear family. The less older people have to be treated as problems or burdens, the more they will be welcomed back and the immensely valuable grandparent relationship will be reaffirmed. With luck, this will also increase family members' concern when grandparents are less fit. If children are routinely in the presence of older people, they will be less likely to fall into the appalling habit of seeing old age as no more than death's lobby.

Third, those two previous factors may, finally, eliminate the unspoken calculus from our imaginations. It is all too easy, in our present climate to believe that the arc of life is, in fact, an asymmetric pyramid – on one side, a steep rise to a peak somewhere in the teenage years and then, on the other, a long, shallow slope to death – and that, therefore, our hours and days become, with time, increasingly less valuable.

The truth is that the human experience is as irreducible at 84 as it is at 14 and, once that truth is accepted, then it becomes impossible to discriminate against, condescend to, fear or be made anxious by the spectacle of older people. It becomes necessary to view people who are full of years not as The Old, some separate, not-quite-human category, but as people, people exactly like us.

And when that happens in the imaginations of enough people, the youth-crazed tide will have turned and, not as individuals but as a society, we really will be 'worth it'.

Five things we can do now

1. Outlaw the rules that stop people taking part in leisure activities.
2. Make media organisations challenge their own ageism.
3. Recognise the market opportunities in the ageing consumer army.
4. Grip the awkward issues out there; tackle the taboo on the subject of dying.
5. To the barricades, boomers!

Notes

[1] Victor, C., Bowling, A., Bond, J. and Scambler, S. (2003) *Loneliness, social isolation and living alone in later life*, Swindon: ESRC.

[2] ONS (Office for National Statistics) (2008) *Internet access 2008: Households and individuals*, London: ONS.

[3] Thane, P. (ed) (2005) *The long history of old age*, London: Thames & Hudson, 2005, p 9.

[4] HSBC (2007) *The future of retirement: The new old age* (www.hsbc.com/1/2/retirement/future-of-retirement).

[5] Goldman Sachs (2006) (www.gs.com/insight/research/reports/report6.html).

SEVEN

Why is ageing so unequal?

Alan Walker

National characteristics

So far, this book has catalogued the extent of unequal ageing in Britain and its impact on older people. It falls to this chapter to try to explain the apparent paradox of the co-existence of great wealth and extreme poverty in old age in a society that is not only one of the most economically advanced in the world but one which also has a long, often radical, tradition favouring civil rights, citizenship and equality – a tradition which united British people both in wartime and in the post-war construction of society and the welfare state and which is witnessed continuously in, for example, the very high levels of support for the National Health Service (NHS). Of course this co-exists, uneasily, with another British trait: our seemingly insatiable urge as a people to create status differentials.

What is 'unacceptable'?

Some would argue, therefore, that inequality is inevitable in a late modern or post-modern society in which status has replaced class as the defining characteristic of identity; still others that, in the age of globalisation, it is impossible to do anything about it, even if we wanted to. I do not share these views. Thomas Scharf (in Chapter Two) used the label 'critical gerontologists' for those in the ageing field who accept neither the inevitability of poverty in old age nor the existence of unequal ageing. For us, there is a moral as well as a scientific imperative to tackle unacceptable inequalities among all age groups including older people. 'What are "unacceptable inequalities"?' the sceptics will enquire. The answer is simple: it is those inequalities that either transgress a distributional notion of social justice or damage the health and well-being of those at the bottom of the stratification hierarchy. The sceptics are persistent, and will press me on 'distributional notion of social justice' and 'damage to health and well-being'. On the former, this idea of social justice means that everyone in the same society has the right, the human right, to enjoy at least the generally accepted basic living standard; on the latter, the scientific evidence is overwhelming that inequality inflicts harm not only on individuals[1] but also on society as a whole.[2] Again the sceptics will come back: how do you know what is 'generally accepted'? Again the answer is rooted in extensive scientific evidence that has demonstrated a national (and international) consensus on what constitutes a decent standard of living.[3]

Individualism and genes

In Britain it is impossible to ignore the naysayers on action to combat poverty and inequality because they are legion and powerful, and they will always fall back on the individualistic strand in British identity recently reawakened and celebrated. For example, the causes of inequality are attributed to 'natural' or inherited differences between human beings. The perennial discourse about the so-called 'underclass' is the best-known version of this thesis, although its last reincarnation was due to a US import rather than home-grown.[4] The familiar argument is that some people are born with natural talents for industry and entrepreneurship, which others lack, and this explains why they end up in different positions. However compelling this may be to what Galbraith called 'the comfortable', because, in the words of C. Wright Mills,[5] 'people with advantages are loath to believe that they just happen to be people with advantages', there is no evidence to support it. In fact, genetic inheritance plays a very minor role in determining life chances – only about 25 per cent with regard to the cause of death after the age of 30, for example. The major players are 'environmental' factors such as income, wealth, social class, education and so on.[6] Hence, those who are offended by unequal ageing, whose numbers include not only the critical gerontologists and the ageing lobby representing older people but, also, much of the general public, must pursue its causes and try to persuade those in political power to implement the policies necessary to create a decent old age for all, instead of just some. This does not mean the *same* old age for all, to dismiss another favoured canard of the naysayers, but rather one that is richly diverse yet not disfigured by gross inequalities.

The causes of unequal ageing

Explaining the causes of unequal ageing requires that we focus on the life course, because older people first of all carry into retirement and, on and on, into late old age a position in the socio-economic structure that is forged at earlier stages of their lives. Retirement itself has an impact on this process, particularly on economic status and the resources that go with it, but the prior life course is the primary determinant of the unequal structure of income and wealth between different groups of older people. It is fair to say that we do not yet fully understand how all of the potential influences on life course development interact with genetic factors to produce particular outcomes, because the necessary data have either not been available or have not yet been analysed from the multidisciplinary perspective necessary to uncover these relationships.

Accumulation

New evidence is emerging continuously, however, and will be expanded by the growing number of longitudinal data sets such as the English Longitudinal Study of Ageing (ELSA) and the Survey of Health, Ageing and Retirement in Europe (SHARE). On the basis of what is secure scientific knowledge it is helpful to think of a person's life course as an accumulation of advantages and disadvantages, from birth to death. Many caveats need to be entered to prevent an over-simplistic interpretation of this proposition – too many to dwell on here. As examples only, life course influences are reacted to differently in different circumstances and by different people, and we know little of the causes of these different outcomes; certainly the role of individual agency must be accounted for in any more fully developed life course theory of causation; and the impact of traumatic events such as accidents leading to disablement must be factored into the equation.

Despite the extensive caveats there is enough evidence to support the notion of cumulative advantage and disadvantage in terms of both biological and socio-economic status.[7] This starts before birth with parental social class, income, wealth and educational levels: some being born with the proverbial silver spoon in their mouths, others not. Such influences are felt immediately in early childhood but, critically for this narrative, they may also have long-lasting effects. For example, clinically significant increases in systolic blood pressure are found among those in early old age who grew slowly when they were children.[8]

Early years

In terms of schooling and attainment, where there is a vast amount of evidence, the striking fact is that not only do disadvantaged young children start school in this position but those with similar levels of competence actually diverge, as they progress through schooling, according to their social class backgrounds.[9] The impact of parental social class on educational attainment is stark: those from higher professional families are more than twice as likely to gain five or more GCSEs at grades A*–C than those from routine manual families (77 per cent compared with 32 per cent).[10] The long-term consequences of these early life inequalities can be seen by the fact that, among those aged 75 and over, one in four who were in managerial or professional occupations have a university degree compared with 0.3 per cent from the routine manual sector.[11]

Mid-life

Early advantages and disadvantages, such as parental class and socio-economic status and formal education, clearly have persisting influences but, for this account, attention is drawn particularly to the resources and events of mid-life because these are the immediate precursors of later life. The giants to be reckoned with in this stage are labour force participation, occupational history, gender, marital or partnership status, health and ethnicity. It is these factors too that determine the major fault lines dividing older people and their combination and interaction have been identified as key risk factors for social exclusion in later life.[12]

Obviously, first of all, employment status and occupational history (continuous *versus* intermittent employment, career *versus* jobs) have a huge impact on the resources that older people will come to have command over. On the one hand, there is the level of income and the opportunities it offers to access resources that are critical in later life, such as owner-occupied housing, geographical location and savings. On the other hand, equally important, occupation is the main determinant of pension rights and, in particular, to access and level of private pensions. For example, men from the professional and managerial occupational classes are 1.5 times more likely to have an occupational or personal pension than those from the routine clerical and manual groups. The level of the pensions received by these two occupational classes differs by a ratio of 3.4 to 1. The class differential in access to private pensions is even greater among women while the difference in the level of those pensions mirrors that for men but in a highly distorted way (see later).[13] Thus both access to private pensions (occupational and personal) and their levels are dispersed widely by employment sector, occupational group and hours of work. To a great extent, therefore, unequal later life reflects an unequal mid-life.

Gender

As hinted at already, these structural fault lines based on occupational class are compounded by those stemming from gender.[14] So, on average, older women are much less likely than men to have access to occupational and personal pensions even within the same occupational groups: roughly two-thirds as likely among those from professional/ managerial occupations and one-half as likely in the case of those previously in routine and manual occupations. In the case of both groups the level of their pensions is about half those of their male counterparts.[15] A key factor here is the gender difference in part-time employment: women are more likely than men to work part-time and part-time employees are much less likely than full-time ones to have a right to a private pension.

As well as hours worked, however, other factors such as interrupted earnings, caring responsibilities and discrimination should be taken into account in explaining the gender disparity in private pension rights (see later). Rather than counteracting these market-based inequalities the state system, to a large extent, has reinforced them. Not surprisingly, therefore, only one in three newly retired women receive a full basic state pension (BSP) and the vast majority of pensioners receiving means tested benefits and living below the relative income poverty line are women.[16] In other words there are systemic, as opposed to individual, reasons why women are more likely than men to be poor in old age and to experience social exclusion and, also, why low incomes and state benefit receipt in later life are strongly associated with multiple exclusion.[17]

Partnership status

Another influential factor in determining access to income and assets, including private pensions, is partnership status, although this fault line spans both mid- and late life. Hence, married/cohabiting, widowed and divorced/separated older women are less likely than their male counterparts to be in receipt of a private pension and, also, less likely than single women. For example, only 28 per cent of married/cohabiting women aged 65 and over receive a private pension compared with 70 per cent of such men. For those of 65–plus who are separated the difference is 36 per cent (women) compared to 57 per cent (men).

Inequality in pensions

It is difficult to overestimate the influence of these differences in access to private pensions in the creation of the main disparities between older people discussed in this book. Built in mid-life, they form the cornerstone of unequal ageing. The unequal distribution of private pensions wealth is truly remarkable: while the state pension is dominant in the bottom half of the pension wealth distribution table it then begins to be outstripped by private provision, especially final salary or defined benefit occupational pension wealth, until the richest tenth, where other forms of pension rights exceed that of the state by about eight times.[18]

Health, class and life expectancy

Another important cause of unequal ageing, which interacts with other factors, especially occupational class, is health. It is in mid-life that the relationship between socio-economic status, occupation and health becomes more apparent than at earlier stages of the life course. After decades of unequal exposure to stress factors and risks the cumulative effects of differences in occupation/socio-economic status on health may be identified at this stage even though their consequences will be felt throughout the life course.[19] Health inequalities stem from multiple sources including differences in occupationally and environmentally based hazards, ranging from industrial accidents to the effects of living in damp accommodation, occupational stress, access to health services and risky health behaviour.[20]

There is still a steep occupational class gradient in mortality, which means that some people do not get the chance to enter later life, equally or unequally, and it is also associated with a range of morbidities. Life expectancy at 65 for women in social class I is nearly four years longer than for those in class V and this gap has grown wider over time.[21] Thus the celebrated addition of 'years to life' is an unequal one: increases in life expectancy have occurred at different rates across the social classes since the 1950s.

Among civil servants, after retirement, an 86 per cent rise in mortality has been observed among men in the lowest grade compared to the highest.[22] With regard to morbidity, older people previously in unskilled occupations are twice as likely to have moderate or greater levels of disability as those from higher-level occupations.[23] Health inequalities, conversely, have an impact on socio-economic status from mid-life, as their effects begin to limit the capacity of some people to remain in full-time employment or drive them out of the labour force permanently.[24]

Ethnicity

No account of unequal ageing would be complete without the inclusion of ethnicity because, in the UK, this is yet another enduring fault line in society that leads to huge material disparities. Table 7.1 contrasts, first of all, the employment status of those aged 30–65 in different minority ethnic groups with their white majority counterparts.

Table 7.1: Economic activity and occupational class by ethnic group (%)

	Caribbean	Indian	Pakistani	Bangladeshi	Chinese	White minority	White English
Employed							
Men aged 50–65	42	57	31	16	62	47	63
Men aged 30–49	74	86	78	55	88	84	88
Occupational class, men aged 50–65							
I/II	12	37	26	9	49	43	39
III nm	8	9	12	4	1	6	8
III m	53	27	29	39	35	30	36
IV/V	27	27	33	48	15	20	17

Note: The above table reflects a social classification system that has now been superseded:
I = professional, II = intermediate, III = skilled (nm = non-manual, m = manual), IV = partly skilled, V = unskilled.

Source: Nazroo, J. (2004) 'Ethnic disparities in ageing health: what can we learn from the UK?', in N. Anderson, R. Bulato and B. Cohen (eds) *Critical perspectives on racial and ethnic differentials in later life*, Washington, DC: National Academy Press

In the pre-pensions age group (50–65) the proportion who are not in paid employment is higher for all of the minority ethnic groups than for the white English group. The non-employment rates among Pakistani and Bangladeshi men are particularly high (69 per cent and 84 per cent). Even at the younger ages, for which employment rates are generally high, the Bangladeshi rate is strikingly low. As far as the occupational class distribution is concerned, on the one hand, the white English, white minority and Indian profiles look similar, with the Chinese one somewhat higher in the classification system but, on the other hand, the Caribbean, Pakistani and Bangladeshi men are lower in occupational classification. Among women of working age about a quarter of Caribbean, white minority and white English women are not active economically, compared with just over a third of Indian and Chinese women and about four-fifths of Pakistani and Bangladeshi women. Among those aged 50–60, only two per cent of Bangladeshi women are in paid employment compared with some 10 per cent of Pakistani women, just over a third of Indian women and nearly two-thirds of Caribbean, white minority and white English women.[25]

It goes without saying, almost, that these occupational disparities translate directly into income inequalities and the picture is a dramatic one. Using equivalised household income for those aged 50 and over about three out of ten in the white groups are in the bottom third of the income distribution table. For the Caribbean and Indian groups, it is more than one in every two, for the Pakistani group, nearly four in every five, and among the Bangladeshis more than nine out of ten.[26] Equally striking is the fact that ethnic inequalities in health increase with age: small differences in early childhood disappear in late childhood and early adulthood but then reappear in early mid-life and continue to widen into early old age.[27]

Age and ageism

So far this explanation for the causes of unequal ageing has adopted a life course focus and emphasised the influential roles of and interactions between social class of origin, education, occupational history and class, gender, partnership status, health status and ethnicity. Age *per se* has not been singled out and it is necessary to do so before concluding this section. Age has an impact on inequality in two respects. First, all of the available evidence shows that those in advanced old age are more likely to be poor than the more recently retired. There is a cohort effect in operation here as, successively, each age group has enjoyed a higher standard of living that has included new rights to private pensions.[28]

In addition, however, there is the impact of a range of events associated with later life such as widowhood, frailty and the depletion of assets. Second, during mid-life and especially later life, workers often find themselves discriminated against within employment, in terms of promotion or access to training or, more blatantly, in seeking jobs.[29] The corrosive influence of this labour market discrimination can have a deep and personal impact on older workers, resulting in acute psychological distress and social exclusion.[30] This is why age discrimination must be included within this account, alongside sexism and racism and all of the other cumulative life course factors that exert different influences on different people, if we are to understand unequal ageing, which is the necessary precursor to changing it.

Is it possible to make ageing less unequal?

Despite the economic crisis and the current political battle over public expenditure Britain is a very rich country which could, if it had the collective will, tackle the disparities in living standards that blight the lives of millions of older people. The key secondary question to the one posed above is: how *much* less unequal? In the final chapter of this book Paul Cann sets out some achievable goals for policy-makers who want to ameliorate the worst excesses of unequal ageing. My purpose in this one remains to explain its existence, and the focus on the role of social policy in this section highlights both the limitations of current and past attempts to tackle unequal ageing and why it is that this problem is much worse in Britain than in many other comparable countries. The long-term nature of the problem and Britain's poor performance in international terms suggest that unequal ageing is not the fault of one particular government but a systemic failure. Moreover, it is one that affects all generations.

Comparison with other rich countries

With regard to educational performance the gap between children from different socio-economic groups is wider in the UK than in other OECD (Organisation for Economic Co-operation and Development) countries.[31] Evidence of the UK's poor record in combating poverty in old age has already been shown by Thomas Scharf in Chapter Two: the at-risk-of-poverty rate among older people in this country is the sixth-highest among the 25 European Union (EU) countries, double the rate in Sweden and four times that of the Netherlands.[32] A clear exemplar of long-term systemic failure is the persistence of high rates of poverty among older women: as noted earlier, the majority of women pensioners are not entitled to BSP. Although efforts have been made, particularly by post-1997 Labour governments, to improve the pension position of women and the increase in full-time female participation in the labour market will assist this process, even in the long term some women and an increasing proportion of men will still not qualify for BSP.[33]

Two pensions systems, two nations

The systemic problem in Britain is essentially twofold: on the one hand, the pensions system has been built on top of labour market inequalities, especially gender inequalities, rather than setting out to counteract them, and, on the other hand, the aspirations of the state system have always been comparatively modest. The recent collapse of company final salary, or defined benefit, pensions has highlighted the historical dividing line between relative poverty and affluence in later life.

Fifty years ago Richard Titmuss[34] identified this dividing line over pensions as the defining characteristic of 'two nations' in old age. The defined benefit scheme is now in 'serious and probably irreversible decline', according to the Pensions Commission.[35] Moreover, the Commission noted that 'employers' willingness voluntarily to provide pensions is failing and initiatives to stimulate personal pension saving have not worked'.[36] Before the recent collapse in occupational pensions they were celebrated as 'one of the great welfare success stories of the century'.[37] In fact, they proved to be a tremendous retirement benefit for those for whom they were primarily designed: full-time, mainly male, continuously employed, salaried staff on incremental pay scales.

Occupational pensions and inequality

For the growing majority who do not fulfil these criteria, overwhelmingly women, they were simply not attainable or, if access was gained, the years contributed were often truncated by childcare and other responsibilities. Those left out of the occupational system who rely wholly or mainly on state benefits are at the greatest risk of poverty and multiple social exclusion.[38] Predictions of future labour market trends, such as a decline in the intermediate jobs which used to provide a ladder out of low-paid employment and an even greater polarisation between good and bad jobs[39] (with health as well as income and pension consequences), do not suggest that an occupationally based pension system can provide an answer to unequal ageing. In fact, it has been one of the main motors driving inequalities in old age.

The role of social policy

Market failure is a familiar story with regard to the provision of income security at any age, which is not surprising because that is not what markets are for. Instead, therefore, all modern societies look to social policy, especially the state, to ensure the living standards of those with no, or only meagre, resources. Although Britain was one of the first countries in the world to introduce a non-contributory old age pension, in 1908 (nine years after Germany and 27 years before the US), and although the Beveridge report, which was the blueprint for the post-war welfare state, was widely admired and copied, in comparative terms the British system is rather minimalistic. This again is not surprising, given the history of repressive social reform, such as the 1834 New Poor Law, which was excessively preoccupied with the issue of eligibility, lest some of the otherwise self-sufficient might be tempted to claim.

'Topping up'

Even the liberal and compassionate Beveridge had to be mindful of these concerns, as do all present-day would-be reformers, and for this and other reasons he established the principle of a flat-rate first-tier pension that would 'leave room' for further supplementation. In his words:

> The State in organising security should not stifle incentive, opportunity, responsibility; in establishing a national minimum it should leave room and encouragement for voluntary action by each individual to provide more than the minimum for himself [sic] and his family.[40]

Support for this minimalistic approach and occupational pensions, as well as a limitation on the Exchequer contribution to the National Insurance fund, came from the Phillips Committee:

> A contribution scheme cannot be expected to provide a rate of pension which would enable everybody, whatever his circumstances, to live without other means; such a pension rate would be an extravagant use of national resources.[41]

This is the principle that survives to this day and which explains much of the disparity between Britain and other EU countries, many of which took the Bismarckian path of earnings-related benefits.[42] This political choice does not fully explain Britain's poor showing in EU pension terms because Sweden also followed the Beveridge model, but it decided against Anglo-Saxon minimalism and went instead for more generous levels of provision to create a more equal citizenship than in the UK. Back in Britain the critical decision was where precisely to set the level of the state pension and other benefits. For this purpose Beveridge drew heavily on the subsistence-orientated research of Seebohm Rowntree. Hence, there was a scientific justification for the political decision to apply a relatively mean standard of living as the norm. From the beginning and for most of the rest of the last century BSP equated to roughly one-fifth of average male earnings; today it is just 16 per cent and is projected, by the Government Actuary's Department, to continue to decline to 7.5 per cent by 2050.

Despite popular belief and media myth, therefore, the British pension and social security system has never been generous in comparative terms. In fact, the welfare state has not sought to tackle inequality in any concerted fashion. As G.D.H. Cole[43] observed: 'The welfare state is only a way of redistributing some income without interfering with the causes of its maldistribution.' Its founders and subsequent political overseers favoured minimalism and horizontal over vertical redistribution (that is, over the individual life course, not between rich and poor) and it has been successful in this respect.[44]

The challenging goals of vertical redistribution or the prevention of inequality have not been considered consistently by generations of policy-makers, although in the pensions field there is no doubt that the original state earnings-related pensions scheme (SERPS), if it had been allowed to mature in 1998, would have decisively reduced gender inequalities. In this context it is not reasonable to accuse the welfare state of failure with regard to unequal ageing because this is not the task it has been set. What is justified, however, is criticism of the various ways in which the pension policy has reinforced or exacerbated poverty and social exclusion in old age, such as the discrimination against women in the contributory nature of BSP. There is, in other words, a great deal of scope for action of an ameliorative and mildly preventative nature.

Challenging the market?

To go further in pursuit of the moral and social imperative for distributional justice and an end to unequal ageing (but not diversity) will be an uphill struggle for critical gerontologists, those in the ageing lobby and others committed to it. This is because to do so means challenging the primacy of the market in the distribution of income and wealth and, therefore, offending some powerful and deeply entrenched vested interests. As so often, Titmuss[45] put the challenge succinctly: 'To recognise inequality as the problem involves recognising the need for structural change, for sacrifices by the majority' and acknowledging 'the limits of conventional welfare'.

The sheer scale of the changes required, in both thinking and policy, to get started on this road are difficult to convey briefly. It would need, for example, a radical shift of resources towards the prevention of inequalities and the harm they do to people,[46] and a joining-up of all the relevant policy domains that have a bearing on ageing across the life course.[47]

The tax system would need at least as much attention as the benefits system and, especially, its many loopholes and reliefs which produce a perverse, upside-down, situation in which the poorest 10 per cent pay proportionally more of their income in tax than anyone else, while the top 10 per cent pay less than those on average incomes. It would also require the reversal of political and public attitudes towards poverty and its causes that have dominated discourses in this field for more than two centuries. R.H.Tawney encapsulated this necessary sea-change in attitudes nearly a century ago: 'What thoughtful rich people call the problem of poverty, thinking poor people, with equal justice, call the problem of riches.'[48]

Conclusion

This chapter has addressed, albeit summarily, the main causes of unequal ageing. The first part identified social class of origin, education, occupational history, socio-economic class, gender, partnership status, health, ethnicity and age as being especially influential across the life course in determining inequalities between different groups of older people. This does not exclude other factors that may be brought to bear, such as housing and sexuality, nor does it imply that these factors or a combination of them lead to exactly the same outcomes. Ageing is diverse and multifaceted as well as unequal.

Quite simply the weight of evidence shows that these structural factors operating cumulatively on a person's life course are likely to produce negative outcomes. For example, in Blane et al's[49] study of early old age: 'the greater the disadvantages accumulated throughout life the worse the quality of life later in early old age.' They found that positive outcomes were associated with earlier material affluence, which allowed owner-occupation and voluntary early retirement and negative ones with earlier material deprivation, non-owner-occupied housing tenures and early labour market exit via unemployment and chronic disability. Clearly these factors depend a great deal on the way that society is organised in key areas such as schooling, employment and the inheritance of income and wealth. Some societies choose different approaches to Britain's which lead to less unequal ageing.

Thus the second part of the chapter dwelt on the role of social policy, because it is these measures that, in some other countries, are directed at preventing the extreme forms of inequality that are found in the UK and other similar liberal welfare states such as the US. While pointing to the pressing need for urgent action to lessen the most corrosive consequences of unequal ageing, this chapter has also stressed the limits of such measures, which are set by the minimalistic, last-resort nature of the overall British welfare state, especially with regard to pensions and social security, where the focus is on reaction rather than prevention.

Of course we can, none the less, imagine an alternative scenario with more equal ageing because some other countries are closer to this goal than the UK and, after all, social policy is merely a matter of political priorities. To transform the British welfare state, however, would call for a mammoth political and policy effort. If it was ever mounted, five steps would help to eradicate unequal ageing.

Five things we can do now

1. It is essential to be explicit about the social, economic and human costs of inequality. The political decision to countenance inequality discounts its corrosive harm.

2. The Anglo-Saxon welfare model is minimal and often punitive in comparative terms and even those older people that claim all of their entitlements are not able to live very comfortably. A fraction of the political effort devoted to the cost of the state pension should be spent on directing attention to what level of income is required for a decent old age.

3. As emphasised earlier, the systemic character of unequal ageing has to be the target for policy.

4. This means acknowledging that the policy legacy is a part of the problem. The case of gender inequality in pensions was used as an exemplar. Another compelling indicator of the perverse role of social policy in this field is the £20 billion net provided by the Exchequer, in 2008–9, in tax relief to occupational and personal pensions, with an additional £9 billion in National Insurance relief on employers' contributions. Rather than being directed at the most needy these pension benefits go overwhelmingly to the better-off. To put them in context, it would cost £6.9 billion to make BSP universal or £11.7 billion to do this and raise it to the level of the Pension Credit guarantee.[50]

5. A fresh start is necessary, one that aims at preventing unequal ageing and not just dealing with its consequences.

Acknowledgements

I am extremely grateful to Adrian Sinfield and Carol Walker for their assistance with this chapter and to Sarah Counter for her technical support. They bear no responsibility for its contents.

Notes

[1] Marmot, M. (2004) *Status syndrome*, London: Bloomsbury.

[2] Wilkinson, R. (1996) *Unhealthy societies*, London: Routledge.

[3] Townsend, P. (1979) *Poverty in the United Kingdom*, Harmondsworth: Penguin Books; Gordon, D. and Townsend, P (2000) *Breadline Europe: The measurement of poverty*, Bristol: The Policy Press.

[4] IEA (Institute of Economic Affairs) (ed) (1996) *Charles Murray and the underclass*, London: IEA.

[5] Mills, C. Wright (1959) *The sociological imagination*, New York: Oxford University Press, p 14.

[6] Marmot, M. and Wilkinson, R. (eds) (1999) *Social determinants of health*, Oxford: Oxford University Press.

[7] Dannefer, D. (2003) 'Cumulative advantage/disadvantage and the life course: cross-fertilizing age and social science theory', *Journal of Gerontology*, vol 58(b), no 6, pp 5327–37.

[8] Montgomery, S., Berney, L. and Blane, D. (2000) 'Prepubertal stature and blood pressure in early old age', *Archives of Disease in Childhood*, vol 82, pp 358–63.

[9] Feinstein, L. (2003) 'Inequality in the early cognitive development of British children in the 1970 cohort', *Economica*, vol 70, no 277, pp 73–97.

[10] The Stationery Office (2007) *Social trends*, London: The Stationery Office.

[11] Walker, A. and Foster, L. (2006) 'Ageing and social class: an enduring relationship', in J. Vincent, C. Phillipson and M. Downs (eds) *The future of old age*, London: Sage Publications, pp 44–53.

[12] Walker, A., Barnes, M., Cox, K. and Lessop, C. (2006) *Social exclusion of older people: Future trends and policies*, Think Piece, London: Communities and Local Government.

[13] Ginn, J., Fachinger, U. and Schmähl, W. (2009) 'Pension reform and the socio-economic status of older people', in A. Walker and G. Naegele (eds) *Social policy in ageing societies*, Houndmills: Palgrave, pp 22–45.

[14] Arber, S. and Ginn, J. (2001) *Gender and later life: A sociological analysis of resources and constraints*, London: Sage Publications; Ginn, J. (2003) *Gender, pensions and the lifecourse*, Bristol: The Policy Press.

[15] Ginn, J., Fachinger, U. and Schmähl, W. (2009) 'Pension reform and the socio-economic status of older people', in A. Walker and G. Naegele (eds) *Social policy in ageing societies*, Houndmills: Palgrave, pp 22–45.

[16] Pensions Commission (2005) *Pensions: Challenges and choices*, London: The Stationery Office, p 149.

[17] Walker, A., Barnes, M., Cox, K. and Lessop, C. (2006) *Social exclusion of older people: Future trends and policies*, Think Piece, London: Communities and Local Government.

[18] Banks, J., Emmerson, C. and Tetlow, G. (2005) *Prepared for retirement? The adequacy and distribution of retirement resources in England*, London: Institute for Fiscal Studies.

[19] Crystal, S. (2006) 'Dynamics of late-life inequality: modelling the interplay of health disparities, economic resources and public policies', in J. Baars, D. Dannefer, C. Phillipson and A. Walker (eds) *Ageing, globalisation and inequality*, Amityville, NY: Baywood, pp 205–13.

[20] Townsend, P. and Davidson, N. (eds) (1982) *The Black Report*, Harmondsworth: Penguin Books; Wilkinson, R. (1996) *Unhealthy societies*, London: Routledge; Marmot, M. and Wilkinson, R. (eds) (1999) *Social determinants of health*, Oxford: Oxford University Press.

[21] Pensions Commission (2005) *Pensions: Challenges and choices*, London: The Stationery Office, p 149.

[22] Marmot, M. and Shipley, M. (1996) 'Do socioeconomic differences in mortality persist after retirement?', *British Medical Journal*, vol 313, pp 117–18.

[23] Ginn, J. and Arber, S. (1993) 'Pension penalties: the gendered division of occupational welfare', *Work, Employment and Society*, vol 7, no 1, pp 47–70.

[24] Crystal, S. (2006) 'Dynamics of late-life inequality: modelling the interplay of health disparities, economic resources and public policies', in J. Baars, D. Dannefer, C. Phillipson and A. Walker (eds) *Ageing, globalisation and inequality*, Amityville, NY: Baywood, pp 205–13.

[25] Nazroo, J. (2004) 'Ethnic disparities in ageing health: what can we learn from the UK?', in N. Anderson, R. Bulato and B. Cohen (eds) *Critical perspectives on racial and ethnic differentials in later life*, Washington, DC: National Academy Press.

[26] Ibid.

[27] Nazroo, J., Bajekal, M., Blane, D. and Grewal, I. (2004) 'Ethnic inequalities', in A. Walker and C. Hagan Hennessy (eds) *Growing older*, Maidenhead: McGraw-Hill, p 41.

[28] Naegele, G. and Walker, A. (2007) 'Social protection: incomes, poverty and the reform of pension systems', in J. Bond, S. Peace, F. Dittmann-Kohli and G. Westerhoff (eds) *Ageing in society*, London: Sage Publications, pp 142–66.

[29] Taylor, P. and Walker, A. (1998) 'Employers and older workers: attitudes and employment practices', *Ageing and Society*, vol 18, pp 641–58.

[30] Westergaard, J., Noble, I. and Walker, A. (1989) *After redundancy*, Oxford: Polity Press.

[31] OECD (Organisation for Economic Co-operation and Development) (2003) *Education at a glance*, Paris: OECD.

[32] Zaidi, A. (2006) *Poverty of elderly people in EU25*, Vienna: European Centre.

[33] Pensions Commission (2005) *Pensions: Challenges and choices*, London: The Stationery Office.

[34] Titmuss, R. (1965) 'Poverty *vs* inequality: diagnosis', *Nation*, February, pp 130–3.

[35] Pensions Commission (2005) *Pensions: Challenges and choices*, London: The Stationery Office, p 2.

[36] Ibid.

[37] DSS (Department of Social Security) (1998) *A new contract for welfare: Partnership in pensions*, Cm 4179, London: The Stationery Office.

[38] Walker, A., Barnes, M., Cox, K. and Lessop, C. (2006) *Social exclusion of older people: Future trends and policies*, Think Piece, London: Communities and Local Government.

[39] Moynaugh, M. and Worsley, R. (2005) *Working in the twenty-first century*, Leeds: ESRC Future of Work Programme.

[40] Beveridge, W. (1942) *Social insurance and allied services*, Cmnd 6404, London: HMSO, pp 6–7.

[41] Phillips Committee (1954) *Report of the Committee on the Economic and Financial Problems of the Provision for Old Age*, Cmnd 933, London: HMSO.

[42] Naegele, G. and Walker, A. (2007) 'Social protection: incomes, poverty and the reform of pension systems', in J. Bond, S. Peace, F. Dittmann-Kohli and G. Westerhoff (eds) *Ageing in society*, London: Sage Publications; Walker, A. and Naegele, G. (eds) (2009) *Social policy in ageing societies*, Houndmills: Palgrave.

[43] Cole, G.D.H. (1955) 'Socialism and the welfare state', *New Statesman and Nation*, 23 July, pp 88–9.

[44] Hills, J. (1996) 'Does Britain have a welfare generation?', in A. Walker (ed) *The new generational contract*, London: UCL Press.

[45] Titmuss, R.M. (1965) 'Poverty *vs* inequality: diagnosis', *Nation*, February, pp 130–3.

[46] Sinfield, A. (2007) 'Preventing poverty in the European Union', *European Journal of Social Security*, vol 9, no 1, pp 11–28.

[47] Walker, A., Barnes, M., Cox, K. and Lessop, C. (2006) *Social exclusion of older people: Future trends and policies*, Think Piece, London: Communities and Local Government.

[48] Tawney, R.H. (1913) 'Poverty as an industrial problem', reproduced in *Memoranda on the Problem of Poverty*, London: William Morris Press, p 17.

[49] Blane, D., Higgs, P., Hyde, M. and Wiggins, R. (2004) 'Lifecourse influences on quality of life in early old age', *Social Science and Medicine*, vol 58, p 217.

[50] Brewer, M., Browne, J., Emmerson, C., Goodman, A., Muriel, A. and Tetlow, G. (2007) *Pensioner poverty over the next decade: What role for tax and benefit reform?*, London: Institute for Fiscal Studies.

EIGHT

Rewriting the story

Paul Cann

We have acknowledged big strides forward over the past decade. Some indicators of poverty have shown sustained reductions in the number of older people who live on less than a recognised level of low income. Pension Credit in particular has helped many older people carry on doing the things that are important to them.

Likewise, periodic transport concessions since 2000 have helped people enjoy their leisure more and stay in touch with family and friends. Although at 68 per cent[1] the rate of take-up of the concessions is low, and although bus travel is only one part of getting out and about, the concessions have put sizeable sums of money behind policy words, which is welcome.

And the debate about age has certainly begun. There is an alertness to our changing demography and more sense of urgency, evidenced by the increasing volume of articles and publications about ageing. Not enough substance has yet been given to the Prime Minister's declaration in 2006 that ageing was a Grand Challenge facing society. But we are perhaps on the way, as a spate of government strategies and initiatives testify.

In 2000 the automatic uprating of the basic state pension in line with the Retail Price Index (RPI) increased the basic state pension by a mere 75 pence a week. A sleepy Whitehall failed to spot the looming outrage. Raw anger about this paltry award triggered a knee-jerk reaction of substantial uplift to pensions and allowances thereafter. But it also activated a sense of indignant entitlement. It is hard to imagine such official torpor now.

But big inequalities remain. And this story is either untold or told in shocking, rapid glimpses which produce shocked and hasty responses, without changing the reality.

Some are part of the biological script of old age. The risks of stroke, cognitive decline, immune system deficiency, bladder and bowel weakening or bone thinning all accelerate in later life. And while research is making important inroads in these areas, ageing research needs far more investment to unearth causes of decline, and thence solutions.

Some we have manufactured and find them too expensive to remove. There can be no moral justification, for example, for the overnight loss of entitlement to claim mobility benefits at 65 (described here by Malcolm Dean in Chapter One), as the benefits available go downhill from Disability Living Allowance to Attendance Allowance. But some we make afresh every day in the way care is funded and delivered, in the clothes we make or our behaviour.

It is time to heed the damage of inequality. As has been graphically demonstrated,[2] evidence clearly points to the destructive effect on communities and societies of widely different outcomes and situations. We have sought to show how those are big gaps, between different groups of older people and between older and younger age groups.

Technical fixes

We have explored several key dimensions of public policy, from the basics of shelter and food to the pursuits and pleasures that make life worth living. There are actions that could be taken now in each area of our daily lives to make a powerful difference.

Take the headache of not having enough cash. The government's approach to targeting the poorest older people has been in place for long enough for its effectiveness to be judged. And as we have acknowledged, there are far fewer people living their later lives on very low income than there otherwise would have been. Yet despite tireless (verging on desperate) efforts using different media and methods, the gap between entitlement and take-up remains by any estimate unacceptably large. We have reached a decision point.

The chasm of unclaimed Pension Credit, Council Tax Benefit and Housing Benefit cannot be closed by will power and well meaning. As long as targeting of help continues, automatic payment of benefits will be essential if we are to make a bigger dent in the problem. And we must all – media, charities, politicians of all hues, the public – swallow the uncomfortable necessity of data-sharing between organisations if we are to identify, and get money into the hands of, the individuals who, we are 99 per cent sure, are so entitled.

This calls for responsible and mature leadership from campaigners, and in circumstances like this toning down the language. Easy polemics against 'means-testing', with its emotive throwback to the utterly different regime of the 1930s, does not help navigate routes to entitlement. We share an obligation to fulfil rights in reality, and where political courage is needed to drive through data-sharing we should back it.

Or take the humiliation experienced by so many older people at their frailest moments. There is now an opportunity, especially for the newly formed Care Quality Commission, to place the all-important area of dignity at the heart of its inspection and regulation regime. This should not be done in a tokenistic fashion, or in haste and under pressure as an item or two in a crowded questionnaire, but adopted as a sacred core value, taken apart piece by piece, examining each of the components we know are part of this human experience we call dignity: from freedom from pain, to access to the basics of toileting and eating properly, to a sense of control and to the experiences that make us feel human and retain our sense of 'self', through communication and meaningful activity. The work has been done to create this framework.[3] It should now be brought on board.

Each of the steps we urge in previous chapters is badly needed. But by themselves they are not enough. *Unequal ageing* is a story whose chapters relate to each other. Poverty is associated with poorer health. Decent housing helps one's physical health. Quality of neighbourhood drives well-being. Most of the determinants of physical and mental health lie outside the system of formal healthcare. Hence the need to redefine healthcare altogether and all the related and artificial territories and their boundaries.

At the same time, imagery and iconography shape attitudes towards age and therefore policies, and they are in turn shaped by fundamental instincts of, at the negative end of the spectrum, fear, revulsion, suspicion, contempt or indifference.

We need to step back from the picture to see its true perspectives and patterns. And in order to improve the patterning of experiences in later life, we need to construct something akin to the approach of the Social Exclusion Unit (SEU), which defined its remit as tackling *a combination of linked problems*, from unemployment to poor housing and health to crime and so on. The Unit has passed into history but at its best it created a strong model for getting change through political patronage and better coordination across government. With a coherent and visionary report on services for older people,[4] building promptly on the preceding and equally promising government strategy for an ageing society,[5] SEU offered a clear map for radical progress, only to pass out of existence shortly after publication and for the momentum to slow as a result – a recurring Whitehall failing in implementing policy.

What older people crave now is an agenda for ageing that does not get blown hither and thither with changing political nameplates and the career roundabouts of temporary champions. And this agenda needs to bring together the technical fixes and reforms, within a shared script, written with indelible ink.

The same stories

Renewed efforts at better co-ordination of initiatives and services could save a lot of wasted energy and achieve a breakthrough in service quality. We list below half a dozen themes that play through the accounts of money, home, place, health, identity and quality of life. Now is the time to act so that, for example, tackling the deficit in housing also addresses the gap in health. Rarely does such action demand lots of new money. So often it is about working across bureaucratic walls, acting sooner, leading better and not losing interest, and using money more in line with what people say they actually want. The themes are not esoteric.

Helping people make sense of their rights and options

Grappling with officialdom is daunting for all of us, but how much more so when we have something which disables us – whether that be an initial frailty or need, natural diffidence, unfamiliarity with jargon, sensory impairment or, all too often, a combination of these. With the help of champions such as the Plain English Campaign we have come a long way since the 40-page Minimum Income Guarantee application form. But despite that, the figures quoted in this book show the enduring magnitude of the challenge of explaining rights and choices. And it applies across the board: the need for good information and advice services has been stressed and promoted across pensions, housing, health and social care services, and so on.

In the best services, however, integration is happening. The recent evaluation[6] of the government's strategy for joined-up services, LinkAge Plus, offers further evidence that it is quite possible to co-ordinate the offer and very popular when this is done. For example, in the inner city a single access point to services for people aged 50 and over has been created in the Tower Hamlets initiative to set up five community network centres, while in the rural context of Gloucestershire the innovation of 30 village agents, supported by a web-based gateway, means easier access to information and signposting to services that are needed. From the eight pilot local authority areas it is becoming clear that the vision of *A sure start to later life* is an efficient way of helping people to make sense of their lives and their choices.

Above all, the public spending implications of doing this are modest. The government elected in 2010 will have an attractive opportunity to transform the quality of information and people's empowerment. To bring together the information, advice and advocacy services offered by public and voluntary sector agencies is likely to cost no more than £1 million in each area, thereby capitalising on the huge asset of voluntary and donated resource.

This is a classic example of the government's key role as pump-primer and framework creator. What will be crucial is that initiatives dealing, say, with social care and housing options, such as the recent voluntary sector partnership First Stop offering advice on housing and care options, are connected with others such as LinkAge Plus or health-based advice services. But this is a challenge for design and collaborative working, not for allocating scarce resources. *Mainstreaming LinkAge Plus would be the most practical and potent way of helping older people connect.*

Safeguarding and sharing knowledge, and making it count

The experience of LinkAge Plus, while uplifting, in fact highlights an endemic problem of government and all agencies working for age. In an information-deluged society we are failing to reap the full rewards of our increasing knowledge about how we experience growing older. It is a sign of progress that every week several new reports and initiatives are announced in relation to ageing. But this generates an equivalent challenge: to ensure that this learning travels to all the parts it needs to reach.

We could make a start by holding on better to knowledge we have taken trouble to pay for and discover, rather than allowing such research to fade from view – such as the important investigations of 'prevention' a decade ago (a subject which we are now rediscovering), the seminal work on dignity in care[7] done in the build-up to the National Service Framework for Older People (itself often forgotten and in disuse), or the bold experiments in mid-life health and well-being reviews[8] which demonstrated the value of acting sooner to avert health crises later, but has slipped off policy-makers' radar. These three pioneering projects are mere examples of the way in which learning seeps through our hands and our collective organisational memory fails to remind us that we already know a lot of the answers.

So it is ironic that the very initiative designed to maximise the retention and use of knowledge about ageing has itself withered on the vine. The recommendation of the government strategy *Opportunity Age* for an observatory on ageing could have amounted to an imaginative attempt at capturing insights and learning, and placing them at the disposal of policy-makers. But the proposal disappeared without trace within the labyrinthine corridors of power, along with a good deal of the energy of that strategy, as the recent review of its progress[9] found.

Yet a dynamic knowledge-gatherer and evangelist of learning is undoubtedly needed, if only to prevent the government machine from going round in circles. The Centre for Policy on Ageing has certainly played a similar role in the past, but is currently under-resourced to fulfil the global networking of age knowledge that is now called for. The new charity formed from the merger of Help the Aged and Age Concern England in 2009 also has a potential role. The UK Age Research Forum, which gathers together the main funders of ageing research – the Wellcome Trust, research councils, government, charities – has made some concrete contributions to knowledge-sharing. But now it needs to move on, to build more bridges between funders, researchers and those who will act on research to improve lives day by day.

A public service for well-being: prevention rather than cure

We have argued, especially in Chapter Three on health and well-being, that there is an urgent need to break out of current structures of delivery that perpetuate old ways of doing things. There is violent agreement across the community of ageing that maintaining well-being and acting 'upstream' is an urgent priority. Indeed, the re-found Holy Grail of 'prevention' has received a helpful push in that direction with the imperative within the recent government concordat on 'personalisation'[10] for a five per cent resource reallocation from health services to community care.

The 2009 government Green Paper on social care heralds at least the chance of change in the way we enable people with needs for some form of extra help to live their lives. Self-directed support and its variously termed sibling initiatives are now the lead act. This is fine and to be embraced, providing we accompany the policy thrust with: the right organisation of services; enabling advocacy that will make such empowerment feasible for people at their frailest and least secure (the early feedback from older people sounded a note of caution about this);[11] and above all the deep-seated 'hearts and minds' change across those bodies and from those people who have hitherto made the running in deciding what is on offer.

In the first place, we need to send the signal through language and organisation. A 'well-being service' may smite the ear strangely at first but it is the right message and it needs to be championed. By the same token, Lord Layard's foray[12] to send public policy in to grapple with the subject of happiness attracted its critics, but was entirely sound in focusing on the things that matter most to people and on practical strategies for putting happiness within reach, such as talking therapies.

The debate about ways of funding social care will move steadily forward, accelerated it is to be hoped by the current government initiative. What is of fundamental importance is that we together design and develop local configurations of accountable agencies, commissioning new, relevant services from independent, regulated providers. These should have as their mission the promotion of well-being and should break out of the rut of the status quo. This transition has to be engineered without destabilising services that have a value and will continue to have some value. But for there to be real change in the range and relevance of the offer the direction will have to be signalled from the outset.

As Anna Coote argued in Chapter Three, a bias towards maintaining health demands much more alertness to, and action to avert, health threats. This requires more decisive action early enough in the life course, which in turn means much more systematic alignment between age interests and the other protagonists across the life course. In particular, the link is central with the Equality and Human Rights Commission (EHRC) and its work on lifelong hazards to fairness.[13]

And the most powerful point of influence on that life course for agencies concerned with later life is the so-called mid-life. As noted previously there are precedents for effective intervention as people turn 50 or thereabouts, to detect likely health problems and to take action. This model has great potential to improve lives, especially those of the most disadvantaged. To be fair, the government has now acted. The health 'MOT' is now to be offered from the age of 40 onwards. The planned vascular checks are much to be welcomed. The prevention package is in its initial roll-out and subsequent additional services will help a lot.

But we, as empowered, well-informed individuals, could do so much more here. We should now have the vision to take the principle to the next stage, where — with the same breadth of approach as characterised the LinkAge Plus pilots — we enable people at work, at their GP surgery or online, to review not only their health status but at the same time their wealth status, as well as checking out that which could make a difference to both: their skills and employability. *There is now a strong case to test that integrated mid-life review, not only online but also reaching out to the most disadvantaged and seldom-heard communities*, as was successfully explored by the Health Development Agency in its pre–retirement pilots.

The problem of redundancy: a coalition to combat loneliness

'Prevention' is a negative term describing a potentially positive process. Perhaps the condition we most deeply wish to prevent is that of 'redundancy' – redundancy not only in terms of loss of paid work through enforced retirement, but of a whole host of other contributions we are accustomed to making and which define our humanity: to our partner, to our family members younger and older, to our professional colleagues, to our local club, to our street. We approach life as a series of new experiences, gaining wisdom, friendship, possessions, love, yet older age too often reverses the direction and inflicts loss after loss on us, of health, material well-being, meaningful activity, loved ones. And the worst loss of all is arguably loss of meaning and value to others.

The most poignant testimony to this reversal of fortunes is the large number of people who, as they grow older, feel they have been deserted by society around them. Research estimates vary but hover around the figure of 10 per cent of older people who feel cut-off and are without regular contact. This has prompted some leading agencies in the field of ageing to view social isolation as their greatest concern. Indeed, as a welcome response a coalition is being assembled of interested organisations that share the goal of reducing this blight on later life.

However, efforts to remedy a sense of lost value will falter unless they help to rekindle that self-esteem. This can be done only through mutual contribution, and by affirming the principle that people want above all to go on contributing and can almost always do that, albeit in different and subtler ways. Debate about stages of ageing, with notions of an 'active' stage followed by a stage of decline – the so-called Third and Fourth Ages – is dangerous. However much physical decline may create greater dependency, the moment we treat an individual as having passed into the category of dependency is the point at which we definitively reduce their humanity and confer isolation on them. *Concerted work by age agencies tackling isolation should focus on contribution and interdependence.*

Harnessing technologies

A current topic of public concern is the impact of the recession and its limiting effect on social policy and progress. What is missed here and seemed at the time of writing to be largely absent from the government's new ageing strategy is a sense of the economic and indeed caring opportunity afforded by technologies of various kinds. Some cautious steps were taken with the launch of the Preventative Technology Grants – a two-year programme of £80 million of central government pump-priming to local authorities.

The UK is moving from a relatively early stage of utilising the full power of assistive technology, and it is too soon to plot the future trajectory of this dimension of care and support. But leaving pioneering and experimentation to local agencies is not enough. Just as the government has taken a serious interest in effecting as smooth as possible a shift to digital television and other opportunities, so *it should also champion assistive technology not as a novel enhancement of the current offer but as an integral and mandatory part of any care package*, disseminating the encouraging experience of local projects such as the West Lothian programme.

A platform of rights

Across all aspects of daily life runs the obstacle of entitlement: rights that are either not secured in practice or are lacking in the first place. Extensive research[14] has documented the ageism that permeates social policy and practical delivery of goods and services. The government deserves great credit for its announcement in 2008 of a commitment to outlaw unfair age discrimination in the provision of goods, facilities and services. There is now a risk of a recurrence of the Whitehall malaise of lost momentum. At the time of writing, the Equality Bill to implement the commitment was going through Parliament. *The crux of the matter will, however, be the speed of passage of both the Act and supporting regulations.* It is by no means certain that an incoming Conservative government would place the same priority on legislation for equality. This chance must not be lost.

A time for age

Prevailing gloom about economic recession does not inspire hope that the government and society will rush in with bright ideas and new resources to further attack poverty and inequality, even though by objective account[15] the Labour government's track record has been a commendable and long-term pursuit of greater social justice. Eye-watering estimates of the scale of government debt or of the shortfall in public finances threaten to drown out talk of investment and further reform.

These are hard times for the current generation of older people. Some economic pressures or fluctuations hit them especially hard. For example, in 2008 dramatically rising fuel costs engulfed one in three older households in fuel poverty. Cost inflation of items purchased by older people runs at a faster rate than the pattern of spending in the general population.

Meanwhile, returns on savings dwindle and annuity values plummet. And the recession means the drying-up of investment finance for care providers, threatening stagnation in this vital sector and in the quality of care it can manage to deliver. Over the past year two of the biggest care home operators in the country have experienced severe business pressures. It is scant comfort that the slow-down acts as a brake on rates of pensioner poverty (which normally rises as prosperity rises), since as we have shown there are several million older people either side of the poverty line living on very little. So there is little scope for manoeuvre.

Yet now is precisely the right time for a searching look at our priorities. Behind the telephone number deficit headlines there is a far more gripping story. It is a story about our values, and it calls into question what we hold dear.

Over time corporate recklessness in the financial sector encouraged many of us to over-extend ourselves financially. The consequences have often been disastrous but also instructive. Revulsion at greed and irresponsibility in the financial services industry has also made us individually feel uncomfortable. Our indignation has sparked impatience for a correction, for a change of direction of some kind. This in turn has caused many of us to rethink what are truly worthwhile goals and behaviours in life, as exemplified by a drop in graduate interest in a career in the City.

So the crisis has at least prised open a chink through which light might fall on some of our moral and policy debates, such as, centrally, our relative responsibilities as taxpayers to right wrongs and achieve social justice. A kinder climate may be arriving in which to confront possible tax changes, perhaps in relation to inheritance or higher incomes, in order to secure a wider good.

We could achieve socially desirable goals, such as a level of care at the most vulnerable times of life, which we could look at with equanimity, as opposed to the current experience of shocked incredulity as yet another undercover documentary tells things the way they too often are. So this may in fact be a highly formative period for social change, in which a re-evaluation of what matters most leads to change for the better for those who have most need.

The call to leadership

But for that to happen we need leadership – leaders, in our communities, our councils and assemblies, and on our television screens, who force us to look in the mirror, to work through the awkward questions and the serious implications of their answers, such as:

- How is it that we find the abuse of older people less arresting and urgent than the abuse of children, as the case of Margaret Panting (cited in Chapter Five) highlights?
- How is it that we have not marched on the streets to demand an end to indignities of hospital care such as inadequate toileting or mixed-sex wards?
- What kind of environment and personal care do we really regard as acceptable for those we love, and indeed for us, as we lose control of our bodies and minds?
- And why is it that we are so reluctant to talk about the inevitable fact of our death and what we want to happen to us in our final months and days?

We need *leadership* to unite us all behind a mission to end the inequality of ageing, in:

- *Policy:* political leaders deserve credit for the progress made in improving the life chances of children and young people. But the value system is lopsided, even ageist. Like children, older people – at least the oldest old – often lack economic independence, the opportunity to enhance their material well-being through paid work. Their options are more limited, their income more fixed in its trajectory. Now is the time to build on the success achieved for youth *with a resounding commitment in support of age equality.*

  In all of this we hope for a bold strategy from the *Conservatives and other parts of the political spectrum*, whether as the future government or opposition. The prize is spectacular, not only in the well-rehearsed electoral might of older voters, but also via their golden economic asset, which has not been fully articulated or exploited. Longer working and stronger participation offer salvation in difficult times.

But the policy link must be made to what older people want above all – to be left to get on with life, to get out there and on with their lives, not to be tripped up by red-tape hurdles and regulations such as insurance age limits, discriminatory rules on civic duties and enforced retirement, or inhibited by limited social care options and unimaginative marketplaces. There is within the equality issue a powerful narrative of freedom in age and of economic liberalism that ought to resonate well with traditional Conservative values.

- *Markets:* by definition markets cannot be dictated to. None the less, the noise of the approaching opportunity being created by the over-65s, who currently spend over £200 billion a year, is becoming deafening. Politicians can, as noted earlier, strip out the artificial barriers to trading. Charities can promote the interests and wishes of older people to trade. But it is *the leaders in their specific marketplaces who will see the chances*, and end the continual complaints of older people about shops and manufacturers wilfully refusing to open their eyes to what they want and have money to pay for.

- *Culture:* in our popular pictures and stories we express our feelings, including our feelings about age. There are some signs of less suppression of age or fewer caricatures as steady decline and despair. *We need leaders in the media, in our designers, in leisure providers*, who will end the one-sided and pervasive glorification of youth and the silent war of denial against ageing. The more feisty, older figures there are who will live out the maxim that you should never stop contributing, the better. However much your outward appearance suggests dependency, you can give something. You have worth.

- *The movement:* much rests on the capacity of older people and their representatives to tell their story persuasively and realistically. *A vociferous army, loud and proud to be old*, is out there already, both actually (in the form of the National Pensioners' Convention) and potentially from across the whole population of 20 million over-50s. Its challenge is that people do not define themselves by their age. So we may need an evolutionary approach, which, like predecessor rights movements of disability or race, first identifies itself powerfully and defiantly (as age), but then works to cement the common causes with, say, gender, disability, race or anti-prejudice interests. Over time the evolution should surely be towards extinction, where age is no longer an identifier or category. To get there will demand strategic alliances with kindred groups, long-term determination and leadership.

We have told only some parts of the story of unequal ageing. It is not a simple or monotonous tale. There is much to applaud. But there remains too much that offends, too many points and places where we fail in our equality, our humanity or our sheer common sense. And when retirement becomes, as it is literally, a drawing back, withdrawal from society into places of retreat, whether those are ordinary homes, care homes or something else, the story becomes inaudible and the people become invisible to us.

We must not let that happen. We have described technical policy solutions we can apply. We have set out more co-ordinated and collaborative approaches we must organise. But finally, leadership must take the story to a different place, in policy and politics, in the marketplace, in our culture, and from the voices of older people themselves.

So the question now is: who will give that leadership?

Notes

[1] Department for Transport (2008) *National Travel Survey 2007*, Table 5.7 (60 and over), London: Department for Transport.

[2] Wilkinson, R. and Pickett, K. (2009) *The spirit level: Why more equal societies almost always do better*, London: Allen Lane.

[3] Picker Institute (2008) *On our own terms: The challenge of assessing dignity in care*, London: Picker Institute for Help the Aged; Levenson, R. (2007) *The challenge of dignity in care: Upholding the rights of the individual*, London: Help the Aged.

[4] SEU (Social Exclusion Unit) (2006) *A sure start to later life: Ending inequalities for older people*, London: SEU.

[5] DWP (Department for Work and Pensions) (2005) *Opportunity Age: Meeting the challenges of ageing in the 21st century*, London: DWP.

[6] Willis, M. and Dalziel, R. (2009) *LinkAge Plus: Capacity-building, enabling and empowering older people as active, independent citizens*, Research Series Report 571, London: Department for Work and Pensions.

[7] Help the Aged (1999) *Promoting excellence in care: Good practice in acute hospital care for older people (Dignity on the Ward)*, London: Help the Aged.

[8] Pre-retirement pilots, Health Development Agency for the Department of Health, 2001–3.

[9] Audit Commission (2008) *Don't stop me now: Preparing for an ageing population*, London: Audit Commission.

[10] DH (Department of Health) (2007) *Putting people first* concordat, London: DH.

[11] Glendinning, C., Moran, N. and Rabiee, P. *The IBSEN Project: National evaluation of the Individual Budgets Pilot Programme*, York: SPRU, University of York (2008).

[12] Layard, R. (2005) *Happiness*, London: Allen Lane.

[13] EHRC (Equality and Human Rights Commission) (2007) *Fairness and freedom: The final report of the Equalities Review*, London: EHRC.

[14] Help the Aged (2006) *Too old: Older people's accounts of discrimination, exclusion and rejection*, A report from the Research on Age Discrimination (RoAD) project, Open University for Help the Aged; evidence submitted to the Discrimination Law Review, Help the Aged, unpublished (2007).

[15] For example, Hills, J. and Stewart, K. (eds) (2005) *A more equal society? New Labour, poverty and exclusion*, Bristol: The Policy Press; Hills, J., Sefton, T. and Stewart, K. (eds) (2009) *Towards a more equal society: Poverty, inequality and policy since 1997*, Bristol: The Policy Press.

Index